I0024441

Eleanor O´Grady

Elocution Class

A simplification of the laws and principles of expression

Eleanor O´Grady

Elocution Class
A simplification of the laws and principles of expression

ISBN/EAN: 9783742837592

Manufactured in Europe, USA, Canada, Australia, Japa

Cover: Foto ©Thomas Meinert / pixelio.de

Manufactured and distributed by brebook publishing software
(www.brebook.com)

Eleanor O´Grady

Elocution Class

Yours truly
Eleanor O'Grady

ELOCUTION CLASS:

A SIMPLIFICATION OF THE

LAWS AND PRINCIPLES

OF

EXPRESSION.

BY

ELEANOR O'GRADY,

Author of "Select Recitations," "Aids to Correct and Effective Elocution," "Readings and Recitations for Juniors," etc.

NEW YORK, CINCINNATI, CHICAGO:

BENZIGER BROTHERS,

Printers to the Holy Apostolic See.

To Him

FROM WHOM EMANATES

THE GOOD, THE TRUE, AND THE BEAUTIFUL

THIS BOOK

IS MOST REVERENTLY DEDICATED.

" Art is divine in its principles, divine in its essence, divine in its action, divine in its end. And what are, in effect, the essential principles of Art ? Are they not, taking them together, the Good, the True, and the Beautiful ? And their action, and their end,—are they other than a tendency incessantly directed toward the realization of these three terms? Now the Good, the True, and the Beautiful can be found only in God. Thus, art is divine in the sense that it emanates from His divine perfections ; in the sense that it constitutes for us even the idea of those perfections ; and, above all, in the sense that it tends to realize in us, about us, and beyond us this triple perfection that it draws from God.

" Never has an Artist denied his God."—DELSARTE.

PREFACE.

"Elocution Class" is designed to give, in simple language, convenient form, and at small expense, a most thorough knowledge of the fundamental laws and principles of Elocution.

It is the outcome of many years of study and experience. Whilst we retain in "Elocution Class" all that is best of the old methods, we also give the most useful of the laws and theories of François Delsarte.

For although the knowledge left by the great French Elocutionist is fragmentary, we believe we but voice the opinion of every advanced teacher of Art when we assert that every student of Expression should be made familiar with the laws he discovered and the most useful of the many good and beautiful things he has said regarding Art.

We feel certain that this little book will be welcomed, not only by our own pupils, but also by those Teachers and Guardians of youth who regard Elocution not merely as a charming accomplishment, but likewise as a most powerful means to correct faults of carriage, awkward gesticulation, inaccuracies in pronunciation, indistinct enunciation—in a word, all acquired vocal and physical defects.

Elocution as taught heretofore has too often been a blind imitation of the teacher. Now, the fact is, the Art of Expression has its laws and principles, with which every student of elocution should be made familiar. And recitations, instead of being only reproductions of the conceptions and mannerisms of individuals, should be exemplifications of the application of those laws and principles.

Many think that the study of expression makes students self-conscious. This *is* the result if *superficially* studied. But, certainly, *control* of one's powers, which is gained only by study and practice, will cause *self-possession* to take the place of self-consciousness. It also makes a personality more charming by giving one a wider range of expression.

ELEANOR O'GRADY.

CONTENTS.

8   *Contents.*

PAGEPAGE

INDEX TO RECITATIONS.

11

DELSARTE.

Françoise Delsarte was born November 11, 1811, at Solesne, in France. His father was a physician and inventor, but died in comparative poverty.

François, in 1822, was apprenticed to a porcelain painter of Paris, but having great aptitude for music, he sought and obtained admission to the Conservatory in 1825. Here, in consequence of faults in method and direction, he lost his voice.

This seeming misfortune proved a blessing, for Delsarte devoted himself to the discovery of *laws* for expression.

He became a teacher of singing and elocution.

Unfortunately, Delsarte himself wrote no work on art. Delsarte's daughter, Madame Geraldy Delsarte (whom we had the pleasure and profit of hearing lecture), approved of but *one* of the many books that have been written concerning her father's teachings—that by his friend and pupil, M. l'Abbé Delaumosne.

Delsarte was a Roman Catholic, and all his art teachings are in harmony with the creed he so faithfully practised. Delaumosne thus describes his death:

"When he had reached his sixtieth year he was attacked by hypertrophy of the heart, which left his rich organization in ruins. He was no longer the artist of graceful, supple, expressive, and harmonious movements; no longer the thinker with profound and luminous ideas. But in the midst of this physical and intellectual ruin the Christian sentiment retained its strong, sweet energy. Defender of the sacraments which he had received in days of health, he asked for them in the hour of danger, and many times he partook of that Sacrament of Love whose virtue he had taught so well. Finally, after having lingered for months in a state that was neither life nor death, surrounded by his pious wife and his weeping, praying children, he rendered his soul to God on the 20th of July, 1871."

Regarding Delsarte's voice Madame Arnaud writes:

"Delsarte was not without a voice; he had one, on the contrary, of great strength and range, of moving tone, eminently sympathetic; but it was an invalid organ and subject to caprice.　He was not always master of it, and this caused him real suffering."

The same gifted writer relates the following:

Halévy once suggested his singing at the Tuilleries before King Louis Philippe and his family.

" I only sing to my friends," replied the artist.

" That is strange," said Halévy.　" Lablache and Duprez go whenever they are asked."

" Delsarte does not."

" But consider!　This is to be a party given by the Crown Prince to his father."

This last consideration touched him.

" Well! I will go," he said, " but it is only on three conditions: I must be the only singer; I am to have the chorus from the Opera to accompany me; and I am not to be paid."

" You will establish a dangerous precedent."

" Those are my irrevocable terms."

All were granted.

From his youth up Delsarte manifested this, perhaps excessive, contempt for money.　On one occasion it was quite justifiable.　Father Bambini had taken him to a party where he was to sing on very advantageous terms.　The scholar was treated with deference; but the teacher, who had neither a fine face nor the claims of

youth to shield him against aristocratic preju-
dice, was received much as a servant would
have been who had made a mistake in the door.

The young singer felt the blood mantle his
brow, and his heart rebelled.

"'Take your hat and let us go!'" he said to
his old master.

"But why?" replied the good man. He had
heeded nothing but his pupil's success. Delsarte dragged him away in spite of his protests,
and lost by his abrupt departure the profits of
the evening.

We will conclude our short sketch by quoting
an opinion expressed by Adolphe Guéroult
(*Presse*, May 15, 1858) regarding Delsarte: "To
discover and produce wonderful effects is pre-
eminently the characteristic of great artists,
but never, so far as I can learn, has it occurred
to any one, before Delsarte, to attach these
strokes of genius to positive laws.

"The eloquent secrets of pantomime, the im-
perceptible movements which, in great actors,
so forcibly impress us, coming under the observation of this discoverer, were by him analyzed
and synthetized in accordance with laws whose
clearness and simplicity render them doubly
admirable."

TO THE TEACHER.

In this volume we have considered rather the convenience and benefit of the pupil than the artistic arrangement of the matter.

The knowledge it contains will be found quite sufficient for the ordinary student of elocution. But for those who have *years* to devote to the study of expression we recommend the authors referred to and quoted through the book.

All the matter is to be memorized except that within brackets. We have endeavored to make the examples for practice more beneficial and charming by using (in most cases), instead of isolated passages, complete recitations. Delsarte says: " A portion of a whole cannot be seriously appreciated by any one ignorant of the constitution of that whole."

We have left the division of the matter into lessons to the teacher, as the length of a task, as well as its subject-matter, must depend upon the ability and need of the pupil.

The teacher should insist that, during the elocution lesson, no form of garment should be worn which would interfere with the free use of the agents of expression. It is impossible to use the voice artistically if the throat, chest, and abdomen be not left free action.

One cannot tread with elasticity if the elaborate mechanism of the foot be confined in shoes often narrower and shorter than the foot itself. The hinge-like movement necessary in beautiful walking is thus rendered impossible.

The voice should be developed *gradually* and *carefully*.

Lamperti's advice with regard to the singing voice should be followed by every teacher of vocal culture. He insists upon exercising the voice very softly at first; for, he says, if a good resonance cannot be produced on a *soft* tone it certainly cannot be made on a *loud* one.

The teacher should assign an elocution lesson, see that the pupils prepare it, give the necessary assistance regarding its understanding and application—in a word, to the *elocution lesson* give the definite teaching which the other studies receive.

We have found that the teaching of appropriate gestures is a most pleasing way to induce very young students to make the *pauses*, which are so necessary to the proper expression of ideas, and without which the so-called elocution is not only disagreeable to the ear, but ruinous to the voice. No young pupil should be allowed to utter a harsh sound or give utterance to a faulty quality of voice in reciting.

The pupil should be frequently drilled upon the " vowel and consonant " exercises. This elementary work is so often neglected that we feel we need not apologize for calling attention to it here.

INSTRUCTIONS TO RECITERS.

(As most of our examples for practice are also complete recitations, we here give a few hints to reciters.)

RECITATIONS should be selected which inculcate beauty, truth, and virtue.

[Delsarte says: " Beauty purifies the sense, truth illuminates the mind, virtue sanctifies the soul."

And Plato: "The young citizens must not be allowed to grow up amongst images of evil, lest their souls assimilate the ugliness of their surroundings. Rather should they be like men living in a beautiful and healthy place; from everything that they see and hear, loveliness, like a breeze, should pass into their souls, and teach them, without their knowing it, the truth of which beauty is a manifestation."]

Recitations should also be suited to the age, culture, and talent of the pupil.

Upon appearing before the audience the reciter should stand in the position of respect— viz., heels nearly together, toes pointing slightly outward.

Next comes the bow; the title of the recitation is then given, with name of the author.

In speaking to the audience the reciter should turn front, reserving right and left oblique for personating and picturing.

It is very essential that the reciter should see vividly the picture or scene to be portrayed. It is also of importance that, having located fixed objects, he should remember the location. For instance, if a reciter, in the commencement of a recitation, place a tower on his *right*, when referring to it again he must not have it on his *left*.

In *description*, the reciter should glance from the audience to the scene he is describing; but in impersonation he should appear to speak to the *imagined* person and not to the audience. The reciter should be careful that the face express the sentiment he is uttering.

It is the *face* that must decide the real meaning, in many cases, of the gestures made by the hands. For example, the clasped hands are employed to express joy, sorrow, and prayer. It is the expression of the face which interprets and tells instantly which sentiment is meant.

If the recitation be in poetry, the reciter must carefully avoid the fault of letting the voice fall at the end of every line. This is often

done by young pupils, even when the sense im·
peratively demands its suspension.   How many,
in this way, would make nonsense of the following true statement.

> " Every lady in the land
>   Has twenty nails; upon each hand
> Five; and twenty on hands and feet;
>   Nor more nor less, to be complete."

Another common error is changing pronunci·
ation for the sake of rhyme.

Bell in his " Essays and Postscripts on Elo·
cution " says: " Ought a reader to be influenced
by the poet's license; and would he be justified
in changing pronunciation for the sake of
rhyme ?   Certainly not; because to change the
sound is to change the word, and so to change
the thought.   The reader's duty is to present
the intended word in its ordinary form to the
ear, and leave the poet to be responsible for his
failure to match the sounds."

There are, however, some words for which
two pronunciations are given, in which case we
should choose the rhyming one.   For example,
the Century Dictionary gives for the word
again two pronunciations—*a-gen'* and *a-gän.'*

We advise the pupil to pronounce according
to the best dictionaries, and never to change

pronunciation for rhyme unless the authority of some good dictionary warrants it.

Another common error is neglecting the " verse pause," that occurring at the end of the line. This is always to be observed if the *poetic* form of the composition is to be expressed. The neglect of this makes prose reading, destroying the music and weakening the thought.

ELOCUTION CLASS.

DEFINITIONS.

What is elocution ?

Elocution is the art of expressing feelings, affections, and thoughts by the threefold language of tone, gesture, and speech.

What is necessary in order to become proficient in the art?

A knowledge of the laws and principles that govern tone, gesture, and speech, and sufficient practice to give control of the agents used in their expression.

[Delaumosne thus defines the art of expression: "It is the means of expressing the phenomena of the soul by the play of the organs."]

What are the agents of expression ?

The head, torso, and limbs.

What is the meaning of poise ?

It means the state of being balanced. In elocution it signifies the opposition of the different parts of the body according to the " law

of grace" which the genius of Delsarte discovered and which he named the "Law of
Opposition."

What is art?

Art, in its most simple expression, is the
faithful representation of nature.

How does Delsarte define art?

Delsarte says: "Art is at once the knowledge, the possession, and the free direction of
the agents by virtue of which are revealed the
life, soul, and mind. It is the appropriation of
the sign to the thing. It is the relation of the
beauties scattered through nature to a superior
type. It is not, then, the mere imitation of
nature."

[The proof that Delsarte's definition of art is
true is shown by the work of all great artists,
ancient and modern.]

What does Delsarte assert regarding beauty?

That " perfect beauty is nowhere to be found,
and that the artist must create it by synthetic
work."

[Synthesis—the composition of separate elements into a whole.]

He also affirms that " in so far as it responds
to the particular type in accordance with which
it is formed, every creature bears the crown of
beauty; because in its correspondence with its

type it manifests, according to its capacity, the Divine Being who created it."

He also says: " The beautiful admits of three characters, which we distinguish under the titles of ideal beauty, moral beauty, and plastic beauty.

" Plato defined ideal beauty when he said: ' Beauty is the splendor of truth.'

" St. Augustine said of moral beauty that it is the splendor of goodness.

" I define plastic beauty as the plastic manifestation of truth and goodness."

CARRIAGE.

[One of the most important of the benefits to be derived from a course of lessons in expression is the correction of faults of carriage.

And we take this opportunity to caution young teachers to be most patient while striving to correct faults of bearing. Some of these faulty tendencies are hereditary, some others, through long habit, may have become second nature.]

What should be the position of the speaker?

Although the speaker's position may vary, it must always be in harmony with the sentiment he is uttering.

Poising Exercises.

1. Stand easily erect, heels nearly together, toes pointing slightly outward, head well balanced and held midway between the shoulders, chest active, and the weight of the body distributed equally upon both legs.

What does this position signify?

Respect.

2. Stand in first position, then change the weight of the body to the right leg, and at the same time incline the head toward it and the torso away from it.

Shift the weight to the left leg and simultaneously incline the torso to the right and the head to the left.

[The leg which bears the principal weight of the body is called the *strong* leg, and the other the *free* leg.]

3. With the weight of the body on the left leg, advance the *free* leg a few inches—about three—allowing the right foot to rest lightly upon the ground, with the knee a little bent. Practise same with the left leg.

[This is sometimes called the " speaker's position."]

In all positions where the arms are *inactive,* the head leans toward the leg which bears the principal weight of the body, and the torso from it.

The pupil must be careful to shift the weight from the leg before using it, as *ease of movement* depends upon doing so.

[When the arms are *in motion* the opposition is between the head and arms. The torso leans from the strong leg.]

The human form has grace of expression when it combines the elements of ease, precision, and harmony.

RESPIRATION.

Upon what does all good elocution depend?

Upon correct breathing.

There are two kinds of breathing, the natural and the artistic.

The natural breathing is the inhalation and exhalation which are necessary for life. It is the breathing of the new-born infant.

Artistic breathing consists of three acts. First, inhaling or filling the lungs; second, holding the breath; and third, exhaling or sending it out.

Is not natural breathing sufficient?

While natural breathing is sufficient for the

preservation of life, we cannot speak, sing, or move beautifully without artistic respiration.

What is meant by diaphragmatic or deep breathing?

Breathing by the combined action of the diaphragm and the abdominal muscles. It is the act of filling the lungs completely.

Is not this done in natural respiration?

Rarely. The lungs are often but one third filled. For song, speech, and, indeed, for all graceful movement, we need nearly two thirds more.

When is deep breathing necessary?

Whenever full and sustained tones are required.

What is the diaphragm?

The diaphragm is the muscular and tendinous partition separating the cavity of the chest from that of the abdomen. It is a muscle of *inspiration* only.

What is the effect of deep breathing?

By the practice of deep breathing the lungs are enabled to inhale a greater quantity of air and also retain it with ease.

Breathing Exercises.

1. Standing easily erect with the weight on the *balls* of the feet, the pupil will inhale and ex-

hale while counting four, being careful to take exactly the same time to send the breath out as in taking it.

2. Inhale slowly. When the lungs are nearly filled, hold the breath while counting four slowly, then send the breath out as slowly as it was inhaled.

3. Fill the lungs completely, hold the breath while counting five, then emit it.

[According to " Arnaud," Delsarte taught diaphragmatic breathing, and insisted upon the use of the artificial breath. " It is certain that one may sing with the natural respiration; but it is rapidly exhausted if not augmented by additional inhalation; for it results in dryness and breathlessness, which cause suffering alike to singer and listener. The artificial breath, on the contrary, preserves the ease and freshness of the voice."]

The exercise for holding the breath should be practised every day, increasing the time for holding the breath from five to sixty seconds.

CHANNELS FOR RESPIRATION.

What are the channels for respiration ?
The nostrils and the mouth.

Which should be used ?

We recommend inhaling through the nostrils, especially, when we pass from a heated atmosphere to one that is the reverse, and also when the air is impure or the throat delicate.

Can inspiration and expiration take place at the same time ?

No, since all air entering the lungs and all breath leaving them must pass through the larynx. Forgetfulness of this simple fact is the cause of very serious injury to young students.

Should inspiration be inaudible ?

Inspiration should be inaudible and, as far as possible, *invisible.*

Should the lungs be entirely filled when about to speak ?

No. If the lungs be *entirely* filled when about to speak, the first tone will not be under control.

Should all the breath be used in speech ?

It is not well to allow the lungs to become exhausted. In most cases it is best to use only the surplus breath. The painful " gasping " we so often hear is a consequence of ignorance with regard to this matter.

Is not the " gasp " sometimes used as a means of expression ?

It is. " Every quality of utterance that

would be a defect if habitual may be an excellence under appropriate circumstances. Whisper, hoarseness, panting, respiration, tremulous voice, and every other functional affection may find occasion for their manifestation in expressive delivery." (Bell.)

What should be the first aim in vocal culture?

To preserve and improve the natural beauty of the voice.

PAUSES.

Respiration and silence are both powerful means of expression. The student must therefore be carefully instructed not only *how* to breathe, but also regarding the *opportunities* offered to do so.

" In good reading or reciting, every part of a sentence expressing a separate fact or circumstance is given by itself."

A pause may be made after the subject of a sentence, whether simple or compound.

A pause is required between two nouns in the same case.

A pause should be made before and after adjectives following the words they qualify.

A pause must be made before and after

words and phrases which express time, place, or manner.

A pause is necessary before and after a slurred passage.

A pause should be made after *but, hence,* and similar words that mark a transition.

A pause should be made in case of ellipses.

There is a pause required on the last word of a line in poetry, even when the completion of the sense is found in the line which follows. This dwelling on the word has been called the " verse pause." No one can read poetry exquisitely without employing this pause.

[The above suggestions are simply given to assist. The pupil must understand that there are many pauses made in emotional reading for which no rules can be given, as they are not subject to laws.]

[Delaumosne treats of respiration and silence under the same title because of their affinity. Here are some of the beautiful things he says regarding silence:

" Silence is God's speech."

" Gesture is conceived in silence."

"Silence is the father of speech, and should justify it."]

In the following exercise the pauses are marked thus (').

ONLY A SOLDIER.

Unarmed and unattended' walks the Czar'
  Through Moscow's busy street' one winter's
    day.
The crowd' uncover' as his face' they see—
  " God greet the Czar!" they say.

Along his path' there moved' a funeral—
  Gray spectacle of poverty and woe';
A wretched sledge', dragged' by one weary
    man'
  Slowly' across the snow.

And on the sledge', blown by the winter wind',
  Lay' a poor coffin', very rude and bare.
And he' who drew it' bent' before his load'
  With dull and sullen air.

The Emperor' stopped and beckoned' to the
    man:
  "Who is't' thou bearest' to the grave?" he
    said.
" Only a soldier', sire!" the short reply;
  " Only a soldier', dead."

" Only a soldier!" musing, said the Czar;
  " Only a Russian, who was poor and brave.
Move on, I follow. Such' a one goes not
  Unhonored' to his grave."

He bent his head, and silent' raised his cap,
  The Czar of all the Russians', pacing' slow,
Following the coffin', as again' it went
  Slowly' across the snow.

The passers on the street', all wondering',
  Looked' on that sight', then followed' si-
      lently';
Peasant and prince, the artisan and clerk,
  All' in one company'.

Still, as they went, the crowd' grew ever more,
  Till thousands' stood around the friendless
      grave,
Led' by that princely heart', who', royal', true,'
  Honored' the poor and brave.

HERE SLEEPS THE BARD.—MOORE.

(The verse pause is marked thus —.)

Here sleeps the Bard who knew so well
All the sweet windings of Apollo's shell;
Whether its music roll'd like torrents near,
Or died, like distant streamlets, on the ear.

Sleep, sleep, mute bard; alike unheeded now
The storm and zephyr sweep thy lifeless brow;—
That storm, whose rush is like thy martial lay;
That breeze which, like thy love-song, dies
    away.

TONE.

Where does all vocal sound begin?

In the larynx. The tube through which the air passes to the lungs and back again is called the windpipe or trachea. At its top is the larynx, and voice is formed by the breath, in its outward passage, setting in vibration the edges of the aperture of the larynx, the glottis.

How many properties has the voice?

The voice has three properties—force, pitch, and quality.

To what do they relate?

Force relates to the energy with which a tone is given, pitch to its elevation or depression, and quality to its kind.

[The best efforts of both teacher and pupil must be directed to the cultivation of these three properties of the voice, as all the artifices of the elocutionist depend upon them.]

VOWELS AND CONSONANTS.

[After the pupil has mastered the primary lessons on Position, Respiration, and Tone, too much attention cannot be given to drills upon *Enunciation*, as beauty and intelligibility of speech depend upon the perfection with which the *vowels* and *consonants* of a language are enunciated.]

BELL'S VOWEL TABLE.

1. eel;	8. her;
2. ill;	9. up, urn;
3. ale;	10. on, all;
4. ell, ere;	11. ore;
5. an;	12. old;
6. ask;	13. pull, pool.
7. ah;	

U after a vocal consonant is *u* as in duty, literature; *u* after *r* is *oo*, as in rue, true.

Exercise on Vowels.

Give in a whisper ē, ā, ah, awe, oh, oo.

Give the vowel ē, extending the lips side-wise.

Open the mouth to its widest extent and give *ah*.

Contract the lips and give *oo*, as in cool.

Exercise on the " Intermediate a."

[As many pupils fail to give the intermediate ä, we advise, for such, practice in the following exercise. Between ă in at and ä in father there is an intermediate sound marked à.]

Abàft, advànce, advàntage, àft, àfter, aghàst,

alabáster, alás, amáss, ánswer, ánt, ásk, ásp,
áss, básk, básket, blánch, blást, bombást, bránch,
bráss, cásk, cásket, cást, cástle, cháff, chánce,
chándler, chánt, clásp, cláss, contrást, cráft,
dánce, dástard, disáster, dráff, dráft, dráught,
enchánt, enhánce, ensámple, exámple, fást,
flásk, grásp, ghástly, glánce, gláss, gráff, gráft,
gránt, gráss, háft, hásp, lánce, lánch, láss, lást,
másk, máss, mást, mástiff, mischánce, násty,
pánt, páss, pást, pástor, pásture, piláster, pláster,
pránce, quáff, ráff, ráft, ráfter, rásp, repást,
salamánder, sámple, sháft, slánder, slánt, stáff,
surpáss, tásk, tránce, vást, wáft.

BELL'S CONSONANT TABLE.

	Breath.	Voice.	Nasal Voice.
Lips {	p	b	m
	wh	w	
	f	v	
Point of tongue {	t	d	n
	s	z	
	th(in)	th(en)	
	r (rough)	r (smooth)	
	l		
Top of tongue {	sh	zh	
	y		
Back of tongue,	k	g	ng

J or soft *g* = dzh; *ch* = tsh (as in church);
qu = kw; *ph* = f.

Exercise.

["Distinctness in articulation depends upon the application of the following principle: Every articulation consists of two parts—a *position* and an *action*. The former brings the organs into approximation or contact, and the latter separates them by a smart percussive recoil from the articulative position."]

Pronounce *ip*, bringing the lips together and then separating them.

Pronounce *it*, touching the tongue against the upper teeth and then drawing it back promptly.

Pronounce the syllable *ik*, touching the back of the tongue against the soft palate.

Practise *b*, *d*, and *g* in the same manner.

"The initial consonant should be articulated distinctly; the spirit of the word is contained in it."

R is articulated but faintly: 1st, before any consonant; 2d, at the end of any word. In these situations *r* has always a vowel sound, that of *er* or *ir* in the words *her, sir*.

Obscure vowels should be given as nearly like the full sound as one can without seeming pedantic.

Exercise from Bell's " Faults of Speech."

" Prolong for some seconds the elements printed in capitals in the following words, as commonly pronounced: feeL, seeM, vaiN, soNG, leaVe, wiTH (dh), iS (z), rouGe (zh); We, Yes, Ale, An, EEl, End, Isle (ahee); In, Old, On, Use (yoo), Us, Arm (ah), All (aw), OOze, OWl (ahoo), OIl (awee)."

FORCE.

What is force?

Force relates to the energy with which a tone is given.

Name the degrees of force.

For practice in elocution five degrees of force are usually given—gentle force, subdued force, moderate force, energetic force, and vehement force.

Example of Gentle Force.

DIRGE.—E. G. EASTMAN.

Softly! She is lying with her lips apart;
Softly! She is dying of a broken heart.
Whisper! Life is growing dim within her
     breast;
Whisper! She is going to her final rest.

Gently!   She is sleeping:
She has breathed her last!
Gently! while you're weeping
She to heaven has passed!

Subdued Force.

THE NIGHT WATCH.—FRANÇOIS COPPÉE.

Soon as her lover to the war had gone,
Without tears or commonplace despair,
Irene de Grandfief reassumed the garb
That at the convent she had worn—black dress
With narrow pelerine—and the small cross
In silver at her breast.   Her piano closed,
Her jewels put away—all save one ring,
Gift of the Viscount Roger on that eve
In the past spring-time when they had parted,
Bidding farewell, and from Irene's brow
Culling one silken tress, that he might wear it
In gold medallion close upon his heart.

                        In the ranks
He took a private's place.   What that war was
Too well is known.
Days came and went till weeks wore into
      months,
Still she held back her rebel tears, and bravely
      strove
To live debarred of tidings.

Then came the siege of Paris—hideous time!
Spreading through France as gangrene spreads,
    invasion
Drew near Irene's chateau.
Roger at Metz was with his regiment safe,
At last date unwounded.   He was living;
He must be living; she was sure of that.
Counting her beads, she waited, waited on.

Wakened, one morning, with a start, she heard
In the far copses of the park shots fired
In quick succession.

        It had indeed
Been a mere skirmish—that, and nothing more.

          " 'Twould be well,"
Remarked Irene, " that an ambulance
Were posted here."

         In fact, they had picked up
Just at that moment, where the fight had been,
A wounded officer—Bavarian, he—
Shot through the neck.   And, when they
    brought him in,
That tall young man, all pale, eyes closed, and
    bleeding,
Irene commanded he be borne
Into the room by Roger occupied

When he came wooing there.   Then, while they
    put
The wounded man to bed, she carried out
Herself his vest and cloak all stained with
    blood;
Bade the old valet wear an air less glum
And stir himself with more alacrity;
And when the doctor dressed the wound, lent
    aid,
As of the Sisterhood of Charity,
With her own hands.   The officer at last,
Wonder and gratitude upon his face,
Sank down among the pillows deftly laid as one
    asleep.

        Evening came,
Bringing the doctor.   When he saw his patient
A strange expression flitted o'er his face,
As to himself he muttered: "Yes; flushed
    cheek;
Pulse beating much too high.   Phew! a bad
    night;
Fever, delirium, and the rest that follows!"
"But will he die?" with tremor on her lip
Irene asked.

        "Who knows?   If possible,
We must arrest the fever.   This prescription
Oft succeeds.   But some one must take note

Of the oncoming fits, must watch till morn,
And tend him closely."

                " Doctor, I am here."
" Not you, young lady! Service such as this
One of your valets can—"

               " No, doctor, no!
Roger perchance may be a prisoner yonder,
Hurt, ill. If he such tending should require
As does this officer, I would he had
A gentle lady for his nurse."

             " So be it;
You will keep watch, then, through the night.
The fever
Must not take hold, or he will straightway die;
Give him the potion four times every hour.
I will return to judge of its effects
At daylight." Then he went his way.

Scarcely a minute had she been in charge
When the Bavarian, to Irene turning, said:
" This doctor thought I was asleep;
But I heard every word. I thank you, lady;
I thank you from my very inmost heart—
Less for myself than for her sake to whom
You would restore me, and who there at home
Awaits me."

"Hush!   Sleep, if you can;
Do not excite yourself.   Your life depends
On perfect quiet."

                    "No, no!
I must at once unload me of a secret
That weighs upon me.   I a promise made,
And I would keep it.   Death may be at hand."
" Speak, then," Irene said, "and ease your soul."
" It was last month, by Metz; 'twas my ill fate
To kill a Frenchman."

                    She turned pale, and lowered
The lamp-light to conceal it.   He continued:
" We were sent forward to surprise a cottage;
I drove my sabre
Into the soldier's back who sentry stood
Before the door.   He fell; nor gave the alarm.
We took the cottage, putting to the sword
Every soul there.

                    " Disgusted with such carnage,
Loathing such scene, I stepped into the air.
Just then the moon broke through the clouds
      and showed me
There at my feet a soldier on the ground.
      'Twas he—
The sentry—whom my sabre had transpierced.
I stooped, to offer him a helping hand;

But, with a choked voice, 'It is too late,' he
    said :
'I must needs die.   * * * You are an offi-
    cer—
Promise—only promise
To forward this,' he said, his fingers clutching
A gold medallion hanging at his breast,
'To ——' Then his latest thought
Passed with his latest breath. The loved one's
    name,
Mistress or bride affianced, was not told
By that poor Frenchman. Seeing blazoned
    arms
On the medallion, I took charge of it,
Hoping to trace her at some future day
Among the old nobility of France,
To whom reverts the dying soldier's gift.
Here it is. Take it. But, I pray you, swear
That, if death spares me not, you will fulfil
This pious duty in my place."

                   Therewith
He the medallion handed her; and on it
Irene saw the Viscount Roger's blazoned arms.
" I swear it, sir," she murmured; "sleep in
    peace."

Solaced by having this disclosure made,
The wounded man sank down in sleep. Irene,

Her bosom heaving, and with eyes aflame
Though tearless all, stood rooted by his side.
" Yes, he is dead, her lover!   These his arms;
His blazon this; the very blood-stains his!

                  " Struck from behind,
Without a cry or call for comrades' help,
Roger was murdered!   And there, sleeping,
    lies
The man who murdered him!   Yes; he has
    boasted
How in the back the trait'rous blow was dealt.

  "And now he sleeps, with drowsiness op-
    pressed—
Roger's assassin; and 'twas I, Irene,
Who bade him sleep in peace!   Oh!
With what cruel mockery—cruel and supreme—
Must I give him tendance here;
By this couch watch, till dawn of day,
As loving mother by a suffering child,
So that he die not!

  "And there the flask upon the table stands
Charged with his life.   He waits it!   Is not this
Beyond imagination horrible?

               " Oh, away! such point
Forbearance reaches not.   What! while it glit-
    ters

There in sheath, the very sword
Wherewith the murderer struck the blow!
Fierce impulse bids it from the scabbard leap—
Shall I, in deference
To some fantastic notion that affects
Human respect and duty, shall I put
Repose and sleep and antidote and life
Into the horrible hand by which all joy
Is ravished from me? Never! I will break
The assuaging flask. * * * But no! 'Twere
    needless that;
I need but leave to Fate to work the end.
Fate, to avenge me, seems to be at one
With my resolve. 'Twere but to let him die!
Yes; there the life-preserving potion stands;
But for one hour might I not fall asleep?

            "Infamy!"
And still the struggle lasted, till the German,
Roused by her deep groans from his wandering
    dreams,
Moved, ill at ease, and, feverish, begged for
    drink.

   Up towards the antique Christ in ivory
At the bed's head, suspended on the wall,
Irene raised the martyr's look sublime;
Then, ashen pale, but ever with her eyes
Turned to the God of Calvary, poured out

The soothing draught, and with a delicate hand
Gave to the wounded man the drink he asked.
And so wore on the laggard, pitiless hours.

But when the doctor in the morning came
And saw her still beside the officer,
Tending him and giving him his drink
With trembling fingers, he was much amazed
To see that through the dreary watches of the
    night
The raven locks that crowned her fair young
    brow at set of sun
By morning's dawn had turned to snowy white!

Moderate Force.

THE OPENING OF THE PIANO.

In a little southern parlor of the house you
    may have seen,
With the gambrel-roof, and the gable looking
    westward to the green,
At the side toward the sunset, with the window
    on its right,
Stood the London-made piano I am dreaming
    of to-night.

Ah, me; how I remember the evening when it
    came;

What a cry of eager voices, what a group of
    cheeks in flame,
When the wondrous box was opened that had
    come from o'er the seas,
With its smell of mastic-varnish and its flash of
    ivory keys.

Then the children all grew fretful in the rest-
    lessness of joy,
For the boy would push his sister, and the sis-
    ter crowd the boy,
Till the father asked for quiet, in his grave,
    paternal way;
But the mother hushed the tumult with the
    words, " Now, Mary, play."

For the dear soul knew that music was a very
    sovereign balm;
She had sprinkled it o'er Sorrow and seen its
    brow grow calm,
In the days of slender harpsichords with tap-
    ping, tinkling quills,
Or caroling to her spinet with its thin metallic
    thrills.

So Mary, the household minstrel, who always
    loved to please,
Sat down to the new " Clementi," and struck
    the glittering keys.

Hushed were the children's voices, and every
eye grew dim,
As, floating from lip and finger, arose the " Ves-
per Hymn."

Catharine, child of a neighbor, curly and rosy-
red
(Wedded since, and a widow—something like
ten years dead),
Hearing a gush of music such as none before,
Steals from her mother's chamber and peeps at
the open door.

Just as the " Jubilate," in threaded whisper,
dies,
" Open it; open it, lady," the little maiden
cries
(For she thought 'twas a singing creature caged
in a box she heard);
" Open it; open it, lady; and let me see the
bird."

Energetic Force.

(The rôle of Tarleton requires "energetic force.")

THE JOSHUA OF 1776.— W. R. ROSE.

A hoof-beat clatter down the road, a hundred
years ago,
Foretold through Carolina woods the coming
of the foe;

In dusty clouds they swept along, while here
and there were seen

A scarlet coat, a tossing plume, a bit of sabre
sheen;

Well-mounted men, hard riders all, a scourge
by night and day—

The cruel Tarleton and his band were on a wild
foray.

No quarter now for patriot souls, for Tarleton,
in his wrath,

With blazing ricks and ruined homes will work
his cruel path!

The hoof-beats echo far ahead with muffled,
throbbing hum,

Until unto a modest home at last they faintly
come;

Yet though the sound is faint, it brings a
woman to the door

With anxious face, which shows she dreads
some misery in store.

She glances down the sandy road—she sees the
dusty cloud,

With gleaming scarlet here and there—and
then she cries aloud:

"The British, George! They're coming fast!
Unto the woods, oh, run!"

A moment more a man springs forth with pow-
der-horn and gun.

A hurried kiss—a dozen strides—he enters in
    the wood—
The watching woman smiles, and thanks the
    Giver of all good,
And turns and draws a bright-faced boy with
    tender clasp more near:
" My darling child, your father's safe, and now
    we've naught to fear!"
Up ride the sullen British band. "Dismount!"
    the leader cries;
" Surround the house and search it well; we
    must not lose this prize."
With heavy clank he enters in and scowls about
    the room
At burnished pans and tall old clock and an-
    cient spinning-loom.
" Your husband, madam, where is he? Pro-
    duce the rebel clown!
Refuse, and, madam, here I swear to burn your
    dwelling down!
Where is he hid?" She shakes her head. " I
    cannot, cannot tell;"
She turns away to hide the tears that will un-
    bidden well.
" So stubborn, eh? Now mark my words! in
    but ten minutes more,
At hour of three by yonder clock, the torch
    will light your door!"

He turns and calls to waiting men: "Search
    every crack and nook;
And if you fail, I'll start a light may serve to
    help us look!"
He strides up to the window, then, and looks
    out grim and sour
Across the pleasant southern fields, and waits
    the fatal hour.
The woman's eyes are filled with woe, with pain
    her heart doth swell,
And yet between her ashy lips she sighs: "I
    cannot tell!"
The moments fly; then Tarleton turns, the tall
    old clock to see—
"How's this?" he mutters, "time must lag;
    eight minutes still to three!"
Again he gazes o'er the field with grim, un-
    swerving eye,
While softly weeps the hapless dame, and fast
    the moments fly.
Then Tarleton swiftly turns again the tall old
    clock to see—
"What juggling work is this?" he cries; "eight
    minutes still to three!"
He stands and stares a moment thus; then
    strides across the floor,
With hasty gestures, wide he throws the tall
    clock's ancient door—

And there, within the narrow case, that bright-
faced boy doth stand,
Holding above his curly head a clock-weight in
each hand!
Grim Tarleton stares, the mother starts, the
little lad alone
As calmly stands within the clock as if to
marble grown.
A moment thus, then Tarleton roars: "Come
forth, you little knave!"
"No knave, sir," stoutly says the boy, "to try
our home to save!"
Grim Tarleton laughs both loud and long:
"And what's your name?" he cries.
"'Tis Joshua," the little man in accents clear
replies.
"Well named, well named," roars Tarleton,
then—his laugh the room doth fill—
"For though you didn't stop the *sun*, you've
made old *time* stand still!
Take care, madam, of this young scamp; with
such youths at your back,
We might as well give up the fight and take
the homeward track."
He laughs again, and, laughing, clanks across
the cottage floor;
He mounts his horse; he cries "Away!" they
never saw him more.

Vehement Force.

(The cries of the mob are given with "vehement force.")

CIVIL WAR.—AN EPISODE OF THE COMMUNE.*

The mob was fierce and furious.   They cried:
" Kill him! " the while they pressed from every
    side
Around a man, haughty, unmoved, and brave,
Too pitiless himself to pity crave.

" Down with the wretch! " on all sides rose the
    cry.
The captive found it natural to die;
The game is lost—he's on the weaker side,—
Life too is lost, and so must fate decide.

From out his home they drag him to the street,
With fiercely clenching hands and hurrying feet,
And shouts of, " Death to him! "   The crimson
    stain
Of recent carnage on his garb showed plain.

This man was one of those who blindly slay
At a king's bidding.   He'd shot men all day,

---

* From the French; translated by Mrs. Lucy H. Hooper
for the New York *Home Journal.*

Killing he knew not whom, he scarce knew
    why;
Now marching forth impassible to die,
Incapable of mercy or of fear,
Letting his powder-blackened hands appear.

A woman clutched his collar with a frown,
" He's a Royalist—he has shot us down! "

" That's true," the man said. " Kill him!"
    " Shoot!" " Kill!"
" No, at the Arsenal " — " The Bastile! "
    " Where you will,"
The captive answered. And with fiercest
    breath,
Loading their guns, his captors still cried,
    " Death!"

" We'll shoot him like a wolf!" "A wolf, am I?
Then you're the dogs," he calmly made reply.

" Hark, he insults us!" And from every side
Clenched fists were shaken, angry voices cried,
Ferocious threats were muttered, deep and low.
With gall upon his lips, gloom on his brow,
And in his eyes a gleam of baffled hate,
He went, pursued by howlings, to his fate,
Treading with wearied and supreme disdain
Midst forms of dead men he perchance had
    slain.

Dread is that human storm, an angry crowd.
He braved its wrath with head erect and proud.
He was not taken, but walled in with foes;
He hated them with hate the vanquished
    knows;
He would have shot them all had he the
    power.
" Kill him—he's fired upon us for an hour! "
" Down with the murderer! " " Down with the
    spy! "
And suddenly a small voice made reply,
" No, no; he is my father! " And a ray
Like to a sunbeam seemed to light the day.

A child appeared, a boy with golden hair,
His arms upraised in menace or in prayer.

All shouted, " Shoot the bandit! " " Fell the
    spy! "
The little fellow clasped him with a cry
Of " Papa, papa, they'll not hurt you now! "
The light baptismal shone upon his brow.

From out the captive's home had come the
    child.
Meanwhile the shrieks of, " Kill him—Death! "
    rose wild.

The cannon to the tocsin's voice replied.
Sinister men thronged close on every side,

And, in the street, ferocious shouts increased
Of: "Slay   each   spy—each   minister—each
       priest—
We'll kill them all!"

                          The little boy replied,
" I tell you this is papa."   One girl cried,
" A pretty fellow—see his curly head ! "
" How old are you, my boy ? " another said.

" Do not kill papa ! " only he replies.
A soulful lustre lights his streaming eyes.

Some glances from his gaze are turned away,
And the rude hands less fiercely grasp their
       prey.

Then one of the most pitiless says, " Go—
Get you home, boy." " Where—why ? " " Don't
       you know ?
Go to your mother."   Then the father said,
" He has no mother."   " What—his mother's
       dead ?
Then you are all he has ? "   " That matters
       not,"
The captive answers, losing not a jot
Of his composure as he closely pressed
The little hands to warm them in his breast,
And says, " Our neighbor Catharine, you know ;

Go to her." " You'll come too ?" " Not yet."
   " No, no;
Then I'll not leave you." " Why ?" " These
   men, I fear,
Will hurt you, papa, when I am not here."

The father to the chieftain of the band
Says softly, " Loose your grasp and take my
   hand.
I'll tell the child to-morrow we shall meet,
Then you can shoot me in the nearest street,
Or farther off, just as you like." " 'Tis well!"
The words from those rough lips reluctant fell.
And, half unclasped, the hands less fierce
   appear.
The father says, " You see, we're all friends
   here,
I'm going with these gentlemen to walk :
Go home. Be good. I have no time to talk."
The little fellow, reassured and gay,
Kisses his father and then runs away.

" Now he is gone, and we are at our ease,
And you can kill me where and how you
   please,"
The father says. " Where is it I must go ? "
Then through the crowd a long thrill seems to
   flow.

The lips, so late with cruel wrath afoam,
Relentingly and roughly cry, " Go home! "

PITCH.

To what does pitch relate ?

Pitch relates to the elevation or depression of the voice.

How many degrees of pitch are given ?

For practice in elocution five degrees of pitch are given, but the student must remember that the degrees range through the entire compass of the voice.

Name the five degrees of pitch.

Middle, high, very high, low, and very low.

When should they be employed ?

Middle pitch should be used for unemotional passages and ordinary conversation; high pitch to express exultation, joy, and kindred emotions; very high pitch is used in the extremes of joy and grief, and is employed in calling; low pitch is used to express solemnity, awe, and like emotions; and very low pitch the extremes of awe, reverence, and dread.

The following recitation gives opportunity for practice of all degrees of pitch:

ROBERT BRUCE'S HEART; OR, THE LAST OF THE CRUSADERS.—AUBREY DE VERE.

(Abridged for Recitation.)

"This tediousness in death is irksome, lords,
To standers-by: I pray you to be seated."
Thus spake King Robert, dying in his chair.
His nobles and his knights around him stood
Silent, with brows bent forward.   He continued:
" Because ye have been loyal, knights and peers,
I bade you hither, first, to say farewell;
Next, to commend to you a loyalty,
Not less but greater, to your country due—
For I to her was loyal from the first.
She lies sore shaken; guard her as a mother
Her cradled babe, a man in strength his sire;
Guard her from foreign foes, from traitors near,
Yea, from herself if evil dreams assail her.
Sustain her faith; in virtue bid her walk
Before her God, a nation clad with light."
He spake; then sat awhile with eyes close shut.
At last they opened; rested full on one
The sole who knelt: large tears by him unfelt
Rolled down his face: 'twas Douglas.   Thus
      the King:
" That hour we spake of oft, yet never feared,
O best and bravest of my friends, is come.
James, we were friends since boyhood; side by
      side

We stood that hour when I was crowned at
 Scone—
Crowned by a woman's hand, when kinsmen
 none
Of hers approached me. Many a time we two
Flung back King Edward's powers. Betrayed,
 deserted,
By bloodhounds tracked we roamed the mid-
 night moors:
I saw thy blood-drops stain Loch Etive's rocks;
Thy knees sustained my head when, faint with
 wounds,
Three days on Rachrin's island-shores I lay.
One night—rememberest thou that night?—I
 cried:
' Give o'er the conflict! Bootless is this war:
Would God we battled in the Holy Land
For freeing of Christ's Tomb!' Then an-
 swer'dst thou:
' Best of Crusaders is that king who fights
To free his country slaved!' " Douglas replied,
" I said it, sire; God said it too, and crowned
 you.
God, if He wills, can make you yet Crusader;
In death Crusader—yea, or after death."
The King sighed slightly, and his eyelids sank;
Later his eyes unclosed; and with strong voice

And hand half raised as if it grasped a sceptre,
He spake:
" Yon case of silver is a reliquary—
Seal thou therein my heart when dead I lie:
In the Holy Land inter it."

        Three weeks passed,
Five ships were freighted, and the Douglas
  sailed,
Bearing that reliquary on his breast
Both day and night.

       Tempest fierce
On the head of Douglas broke. A Spanish port
With inland-winding bosom bright and still
Received him; and Alphonso of Castile
Welcomed, well pleased, with tournament and
  feast
· A guest in all lands famed.

        The parting day
Had almost come; disastrous news foreran it.
Granada's Sultan with his Saracen host
Had broken bound, and written on his march
His Prophet's name in fire. Alphonso craved
Aid of his guest. In sadness Douglas mused;
At last he spake: "Sir King, unblest is he
That knight whom warring duties rend asunder:
My king commanded me to Palestine!
For thirty days that word was in mine ears

'Neath all our festal songs.   A deeper voice
Assails me now, mounting from that great
    Heart
Shrined on this breast.   Thus speaks it: 'That
    command
I gave thee, knowest thou not I countermand—
I who from righteous battle ne'er turned back?'"
The Douglas drooped his head; a trumpet-peal
Shrilled from afar.   He raised that head; he
    spake:
" Alphonso of Castile, my choice is made—
With thee I march!"   The Scottish knights
    drew swords,
Shouted, "Saint Andrew!" and the Knights
    of Spain
Made answer, "Santiago!"
                  Ere long they met
On a wide plain with white sierras girt
The Prophet's sons, for centuries their foes.
The Moors were to the Christians three to one.
For hours that battle-storm was heard afar.
Numbers at last prevailed; and on the left,
The standard of the Cross some whit lost ground:
Douglas restored the battle.   On the right
His Scottish knights and he drove all before
    them.
The Moors gave way; fleet were their Arab
    steeds,

And better than their foes they knew the
   ground.
Far off they formed anew; they waved again
Their moonèd flags and crescent scimitars
Well used to reap the harvest-fields of death.
Once more they shouted "Allah!" Spent and
   breathless
The northern knights drew bridle on a slope
A stone's-throw distant. Douglas shouted,
   "Forward!"
None answered. Sadly—not in wrath—he
   spake:
"O friends, how oft on stormy war-fields proved,
This day what lack ye? Naught save an
   example!"
Forward he spurred; he reached the Saracen
   van;
He raised on high that silver shrine; he cried,
"Go first, great Heart, as thou wert wont to go;
Douglas will follow thee and die." He flung it:
Next moment he was in among the Moors.
The Scots knights heard that word; they saw;
   they charged.
Direful the conflict; from a hill Alphonso
Watched it, but, pressed himself, could spare
   no aids:
He sent them when too late.
                              The setting sun

Glared fiercely at that fugitive Moorish host;
Shone sadly on that remnant, wounded sore.
Which gazed in circle on their great one dead.
His hands, far-stretched, still grappled at the
    grass:
His bosom on that silver shrine was pressed:
His last hope this—to save it.
                        They returned,
That wounded remnant, to their country's
    shores:
With them they bore the Bruce's Heart; yet
    none
Sustained it on his breast. In season due
The greatest and the best of Scotland's realm,
In sad procession moved with sacred rites
From arch to arch of Melrose' holy pile,
Following King Robert's Heart, before them
    borne
'Neath canopy of gold, and there interred it
Nigh the high altar.
                        James of Douglas,
In later ages named "the Good Earl James,"
Was buried in the chancel of Saint Bride's,
Near his ancestral castle. Since that day
The Douglas shield has borne a bleeding heart
Crowned with a kingly crown.
                        There are who say
That on the battle-morn

King Robert stood beside the Douglas' bed
With face all glorious, like some face that saith,
"True friends on earth divided meet in heaven."

QUALITY OR TONE-COLOR.

["We must know how to give the voice an expression or color answering to the sentiment it conveys."—DELSARTE.]

To what does quality relate?

Quality relates to the *kind* of tone.

How many kinds of tone are there?

Broadly speaking, there are but two kinds—pure and impure.

What is the pure tone, and for what is it used?

The pure tone is that in which all the breath is vocalized, and it is used to picture tranquil emotions and describe beautiful objects.

What is the impure tone, and for what is it employed?

It is the tone in which only a part of the breath is vocalized; it is used to express fear, secrecy, dread, and it is also employed when one is describing objects that would inspire such emotions.

Are there not other kinds of tone used by elocutionists ?

Although, broadly speaking, there are but two kinds of tone, there are others which must be at the command of the *professional* speaker.

Name them.

The orotund, the guttural, and the nasal.

Describe them.

The pure tone enlarged and intensified becomes the orotund. It is used whenever grand thoughts are to be expressed or sublime objects pictured. The guttural has its resonance chiefly in the throat, and is used to express xcorn, hatred, and revenge. The nasal tone has its resonance chiefly in the nose.

[We do not advise prolonged practice upon guttural and nasal tones.]

What is the monotone ?

The monotone—although generally given as a kind of tone—really has relation to pitch and movement.

The monotone is the level movement of the voice. The voice is kept, almost continuously, on the same pitch. It is used to express emotions of awe and sublimity.

Example.

Hōly! hōly! holy! Lōrd Gōd of Sabaoth !

Beautiful sentiments and the description of beautiful things require perfectly *pure* tones.

To produce pure tones, the vocal organs must be in a healthy condition, the pupil must know how to manage the breath so that no portion of it escape with the tone, which should be directed to or placed in the front of the mouth.

[The pupil should give the following exercise, endeavoring to picture its beautiful thoughts with correspondingly beautiful tones:]

THE FLAG AND THE CROSS.

Lift up the flag, yes, set it high beside yon
    gleaming Cross,
Close to the standard of the cause that never
    shall know loss.
Lift praising voice, lift pledging hand; the
    world must hear and see
The soldiers of the Cross of Christ most leal,
    dear flag, to thee.

But wherefore speak of loyalty? Who fears a
    watching world ?
When have we flinched or fled from thee since
    first thou wert unfurled ?
Carroll and Moylan spake for us, and Barry on
    the seas,
And a third of thy sturdy cradle guard—no
    Arnold among these.

And yet they call us aliens, and yet they doubt
    our faith—
The men who stood not with our hosts when
    test of faith was death;
Who never shed a drop of blood when ours was
    shed like rain,
That not a star should fall from thee nor thy
    great glory wane.

O Meagher, Meade, and Sheridan; O rank and
    file as brave!
Rise in your hundred thousands — rise, and
    shame the shallow knave.
Yea, mine own graves, give up your dead,
    hearts strong in battle wild;
Bleed with my blood, wide wounds, once more
    —I am a soldier's child.

Lift up the flag beside the Cross. Will free-
    dom shrink to be
Forever guarded by His sign who died to make
    us free ?
"In this sign shall ye overcome" flamed forth
    from heaven of old;
Yea, in the Cross the weak are strong, the
    fainting heart is bold.

O mother State! O native land! O sacred
    flag! Again

We pledge you sonship, yea, and sword, in sight
of God and men.
The Cross is seal upon our oath, which angels
glorify,
And, soldiers of the Cross of Christ, for you
we'll live and die.

THE OROTUND.

The tone pictures enlarged, deepened, and
elevated feelings through the *expanded pure
tone* or "orotund." This tone is produced by
the descent of the larynx, the raising of the
veil of the palate, and the canalization of the
tongue.

The best direction to produce a *natural*
orotund is first to produce a pure tone; then
gradually *enlarge* this tone. The pupil must
be careful to avoid all harshness.

"Adam's Morning Hymn" gives opportunity
to picture, through *expanded pure tone* or *orotund*, sublime thoughts.

ADAM'S MORNING HYMN.—MILTON.
These are thy glorious works, Parent of good,
Almighty! Thine this universal frame,
Thus wondrous fair. Thyself how wondrous,
then!

Unspeakable! who sitt'st above these heavens,
To us invisible, or dimly seen
In these thy lowest works; yet these declare
Thy goodness beyond thought, and power di-
    vine.
Speak, ye who best can tell, ye sons of light—
Angels; for ye behold Him, and with songs
And choral symphonies, day without night,
Circle His throne rejoicing; ye in heaven,
On earth join all ye creatures to extol
Him first, Him last, Him midst, and without
    end.
Fairest of stars, last in the train of night,
If better thou belong not to the dawn,
Sure pledge of day, that crown'st the smiling
    morn
With thy bright circlet, praise Him in thy
    sphere—
While day ariseth, that sweet hour of prime,
Thou sun, of this great world both eye and
    soul,
Acknowledge Him thy greater; sound His
    praise
In thy eternal course, both when thou climb'st,.
And when high noon hast gain'd, and when
    thou fall'st.
Moon, that now meet'st the orient sun, now
    fly'st.

With the fix'd stars, fix'd in their orb that flies,
And ye five other wandering fires, that move
In mystic dance not without song, resound
His praise, who out of darkness call'd up light.
Air, and ye elements, the eldest birth
Of Nature's womb, that in quaternion run
Perpetual circle, multiform; and mix
And nourish all things; let your ceaseless
    change
Vary to our great Maker still new praise.
Ye mists and exhalations, that now rise
From hill or steaming lake, dusky or gray,
Till the sun paint your fleecy skirts with gold,
In honor to the world's Great Author, rise;
Whether to deck with clouds the uncolored sky,
Or wet the thirsty earth with falling showers,
Rising or falling still advance His praise.
His praise, ye winds, that from four quarters
    blow,
Breathe soft or loud. And wave your tops, ye
    pines,
With every plant, in sign of worship wave.
Fountains, and ye that warble, as ye flow,
Melodious murmurs, warbling tune His praise.
Join voices, all ye living souls: Ye birds,
That, singing, up to heaven-gate ascend,
Bear on your wings and in your notes His
    praise.

Ye that in waters glide, and ye that walk
The earth, and stately tread or lowly creep;
Witness if I be silent, morn or even,
To hill, or valley, fountain, or fresh shade,
Made vocal by my song, and taught His praise.
Hail, Universal Lord! be bounteous still
To give us only good; and if the night
Have gather'd aught of evil, or conceal'd,
Disperse it, as now light dispels the dark.

By lowering the pitch, and still keeping the *tone* expanded, are pictured grand emotions mingled with awe, solemnity, or fear.

Delsarte has said: " Loudness of tone is inconsistent with true feeling. The more one is moved, the lower the utterance. The voice is brilliant when there is little emotion."

" The Closing Year " gives opportunity for practising this kind of tone.

THE CLOSING YEAR.—GEORGE D. PRENTICE.

'Tis midnight's holy hour—and silence now
Is brooding, like a gentle spirit, o'er
The still and pulseless world. Hark! on the
    winds
The bell's deepest tones are swelling. 'Tis the
    knell
Of the departed year.

No funeral train
Is sweeping past; yet on the stream and wood,
With melancholy light, the moonbeams rest
Like a pale, spotless shroud; the air is stirred
As by a mourner's sigh; and on yon cloud,
That floats so still and placidly through heaven,
The spirits of the seasons seem to stand—
Young Spring, bright Summer, Autumn's sol-
    emn form,
And Winter with his aged locks—and breathe
In mournful cadences, that come abroad
Like the far wind-harp's wild and touching wail,
A melancholy dirge o'er the dead year,
Gone from the earth forever.

                             'Tis a time
For memory and for tears.   Within the deep,
Still chambers of the heart a spectre dim,
Whose tones are like the wizard voice of Time
Heard from the tomb of ages, points its cold
And solemn finger to the beautiful
And holy visions that have passed away
And left no shadow of their loveliness
On the dead waste of life.   That spectre lifts
The coffin-lid of hope and joy and love,
And, bending mournfully above the pale,
Sweet forms that slumber there, scatters dead
    flowers
O'er what has passed to nothingness.

                              The Year
Has gone, and, with it, many a glorious throng
Of happy dreams.   Its mark is on each brow,
Its shadow in each heart.   In its swift course
It waved its sceptre o'er the beautiful,
And they are not.   It laid its pallid hand
Upon the strong man, and the haughty form
Is fallen and the flashing eye is dim.
It trod the hall of revelry, where thronged
The bright and joyous, and the tearful wail
Of stricken ones is heard where erst the song
And reckless shout resounded.   It passed o'er
The battle-plain, where sword and spear and
      shield
Flashed in the light of mid-day—and the
      strength
Of serried hosts is shivered, and the grass,
Green from the soil of carnage, waves above
The crushed and mouldering skeleton.   It came
And faded like a wreath of mist at eve;
Yet, ere it melted in the viewless air
It heralded its millions to their home
In the dim land of dreams.

                              Remorseless Time!
Fierce spirit of the glass and scythe! what power
Can stay him in his silent course, or melt
His iron heart to pity?   On, still on

He presses, and forever. The proud bird,
The condor of the Andes, that can soar
Through heaven's unfathomable depths or brave
The fury of the northern hurricane,
And bathe his plumage in the thunder's home,
Furls his broad wings at nightfall, and sinks down
To rest upon his mountain-crag. But Time
Knows not the weight of sleep or weariness,
And night's deep darkness has no chain to bind
His rushing pinion. Revolutions sweep
O'er earth like troubled visions o'er the breast
Of dreaming sorrow; cities rise and sink
Like bubbles on the water; fiery isles
Spring blazing from the ocean, and go back
To their mysterious caverns; mountains rear
To heaven their bald and blackened cliffs, and bow
Their tall heads to the plain; new empires rise,
Gathering the strength of hoary centuries,
And rush down like the Alpine avalanche,
Startling the nations; and the very stars,
Yon bright and burning blazonry of God,
Glitter awhile in their eternal depths,
And, like the Pleiad, loveliest of their train,
Shoot from their glorious spheres and pass away
To darkle in the trackless void: yet Time,
Time, the tomb-builder, holds his fierce career,

Dark, stern, all-pitiless, and pauses not
Amid the mighty wrecks that strew his path,
To sit and muse, like other conquerors,
Upon the fearful ruin he has wrought.

ARTICULATION.

The following lessons on "articulation" embody Mr. Bell's ideas on the subject.

[Defects in articulation should be traced to their cause.

The pupil should be taught the *position* of the organs and *how* to perform the *action*. For as every articulation consists of two parts—a position which brings the organs into approximation or contact, and an *action* which separates them by a smart percussive recoil—it follows that, if the pupil be carefully instructed in both, perfect articulation will result.]

What are articulations?

All actions of the vocal organs which partially or wholly *obstruct* or compress the breath or voice in the mouth are called articulations.

What is the pharynx?

The pharynx is a distensible cavity situated at the back of the mouth: below it is the glottis, in front of it the mouth, and opening from it above are the nares or nostrils.

[When the soft palate covers the upper pharyngal openings—the nares—the effort of expiration sends the breath into the *mouth,* where, if obstructed in its passage, it will collect and *distend the pharynx* to a greater or less extent, according to the degree of oral contraction or obstruction and the force of expiratory pressure. When the oral obstruction is complete,—as in forming *p, t, k, b, d, g,*—the pharynx should so dilate with the momentary pressure of breath that on the separation of the articulating organs the natural contraction of the pharyngal muscles effects the percussive audibility of the letters.]

What are the modes of articulation?

1st, Complete stoppage of the breath by contact of the organs. 2d, Lateral obstruction, and central emission of the breath. 3d, Central obstruction and lateral emission of the breath. 4th, Lax vibration of the approximated organs, in a strong current of breath.

Describe the first mode of articulation— "complete stoppage of the breath by organic contact."

This mode of articulation is performed at three parts of the mouth: 1st, by the lips, forming *p, b, m*; 2d, by the forepart of the tongue and the palate, forming *t, d, n*; 3d, by the back part of the tongue and the palate, forming *k*, *g*, *ng*.

The letters *p*, *t*, *k* have no other sound than the slight percussion which accompanies the act of separating the conjoined organs. The vocal chords are relaxed and the glottis opens, as in ordinary breathing.

The letters *b*, *d*, *g* have the same oral actions as *p*, *t*, *k*; but while the organs are in contact, the glottis is brought into sonorous position, and an instantaneous effort of voice is heard before the separation of the organs.

[It is important to have the power of producing this shut voice with precision. The sound cannot be prolonged, as there is no outlet for the breath. The murmur of voice can last only until the pharynx is fully distended.]

The letters *m*, *n*, *ng* have the same oral positions, but the inner end of the nasal passages is uncovered by the soft palate, and, while the breath is shut in by the mouth, it escapes freely through the nostrils.

[The three articulations *m*, *n*, *ng*, are the only elements which employ the nose in English.]

Describe the second mode of articulation— "lateral obstruction and central emission of the breath."

When the tip of the tongue is expanded and presented to the upper gum so as to leave a small *central* aperture for the emission of the breath, the hissing sound of *s* is produced.

The articulative position of *s*, giving sibilation to *vocalized breath*, produces *z*.

When the tip of the tongue is narrowed and presented without contact to the upper gum or front part of the palate, the passage of the breath causes the tongue to quiver or vibrate, and the sound of *r* is produced.

[In Scotland, in Spain, and on the continent generally, *r* receives a stronger vibration of the whole forepart of the tongue.]

If, from the position *r*, the point of the tongue be depressed and drawn inwards, so as to remove the seat of articulation further back on the tongue and palate, the sound of *sh* will be produced.

This articulation modifying *voice* produces the sound of the letter *z* in *azure*, or *s* in *pleasure*, which, as the *vocal* form of *sh*, may be conveniently represented by *zh*.

[This is the sound of the letter *j* in French. The English *j* has the sound of *dzh*, as in Jew; the voiceless correspondent of this compound (*tsh*) is written *ch*, as in *chew*.]

If the back part of the tongue be now raised

to the back of the palatal arch, leaving a small central aperture for the breath, the tongue will be in the position for the articulation of *y*, as heard without voice in *hue, hew* (= *yhyoo*), and with voice in *you, use, cue, pew, tune, duke.*

[The approximation of the root of the tongue to the soft palate at the back of the mouth gives the last variety of the second mode of articulation. This guttural breathing is not heard in English.]

Describe the third mode of articulation— "central obstruction and lateral emission of the breath."

This mode of articulation is performed by the lower lip in making *f, v*; by the point of the tongue in forming *th* and *l*; and by the middle of the tongue in the sound of *l* before *ū*, as in *lute.*

F is correctly formed by applying the middle of the lower lip to the edge of the upper front teeth, leaving merely interstitial apertures for the breath between the sides of the lip and teeth. The same articulative position modifying vocalized breath produces *v.*

The tip of the tongue applied to the edge or the inner surface of the upper teeth, with contracted lateral apertures for the passage of the breath between the tongue and teeth, gives the formation of *th*, as heard (without voice) in *th*in, and (with voice) in *th*en.

The forepart of the tongue applied to the palate, with very open apertures over the sides of the tongue, produces *l*.

[The fluency with which *l* combines with other articulations has given it the name of *liquid.*]

Describe the fourth mode of articulation— "lax vibration of the approximated organs."

This mode of articulation is produced by so *loosely* approximating the organs that a sufficiently strong current of air causes them to *vibrate and flap against each other.*

When the back of the tongue and soft palate are thus loosely approximated, the relaxed edges of the latter, and especially its narrow prolongation, the *uvula*, are easily thrown into vibration against the tongue, and the Northumbrian *burr* is produced.

When the forepart of the tongue—similarly relaxed—is laid along the edge of the palatal arch, a smart stroke of the breath will set it in vibration, and the rough *r*, as heard in most of the continental languages, will result.

[*R* is called the canine, or dog's letter; but the name is applicable only to the *burr*, which is precisely the same in mechanism as the

snarl of a cur.   There is not much dignity in
this mode of articulation by any organism,
though the lengthened *r* (not the burr) may be
expressive enough in some words, as in the
" rude rolling of a rebel drum."]

THE TUNKUNTEL.

" What is a Tunkuntel ? " he asked,
    " And have you got one here ?
Why don't you let me play with it ?
    And why is it so dear ? "

" A Tunkuntel," I vaguely said,
    " I've really never seen.
Is it a kind of animal ?
    I don't know what you mean."

" Oh, yes, you do!   Don't tell me that!
    You know it very well,
For you always say you love me
    More than a Tunkuntel."

VOWELS.

The glottis produces voice; the shape of the
mouth gives *vowel* character to the voice.

There are two great agents in vowel modification—the lips and the tongue.   The lips, by
their approximation, externally contract the
oral aperture, and the tongue, by its elevation

towards the palate, internally diminishes the oral channel.

[The effect of the labial approximation is the modification of the vowel quality from *ah* to *oo*. The effect of the lingual approximation is to modify the sound from *ah* to *ee*.]

Vowel Exercise.

Ale, Arm, All, At.
Eve, End, Ice, In.
Old, On, Use, Up.
Oil, Out, Ooze.

Repeat the above in slow, moderate, and quick time. Repeat on high, middle, and low pitch.

With rising and falling slides, repeat in pure tone, orotund, and half-whisper.

THE SHADE.

Madame Arnaud, writing on this subject, says:

The shade, that exquisite portion of art, which is rather felt than expressed, is the characteristic sign of the perfection of talent; it forms a part of the personality of the artist. You may have heard a play twenty times with indifference, or a melody as often, only to be bored by it; some fine day a great actor relieves the drama of its chill, the commonplace melody takes to itself wings beneath the magic of a well-trained, expressive, and sympathetic voice. Delsarte possessed this artistic talent to a supreme degree, and it was one of the remarkable parts of his instruction; he had established typical phrases, where the mere *shade* of inflection gave an appropriate meaning to every variety of impression and sentiment which can possibly be expressed by any one set of words.

One of these phrases was this: "That is a pretty dog!" A very talented young girl succeeded in giving to these words a great number of different modulations, expressing endearment, coaxing, admiration, ironical praise, pity, and affection. Delsarte, with his far-reaching comprehension, conceived of more than six hundred ways of differentiating these examples.

Exercise.

"I did not tell you that I would not!"
Say this to express indifference.
Say it in a tone of reproach.
In such a manner as to express encouragement.
So as to express hesitation.
Say "Come here!" as a command.
"Come here," in a coaxing tone.

" Come here," with affection.

" Come here ! " in a menacing tone.

" Come here," to express fear.

." Come here," to express sorrow.

THE TONE OF THE VOICE.

It is not so much what you say
 As the manner in which you say it;
It is not so much the language you use,
 As the tones in which you convey it.

" Come here! " I sharply said,
 And the baby cowered and wept;
"Come here," I cooed, and he looked and
  smiled,
 And straight to my lap he crept.

In the following exercise, " The Lights of London Town," the pupil must picture in the first stanza the blitheness of heart and courage of the " country lad and lassie." This may be done by using bright, elastic tones.

For the second stanza mournful tones should be used.

For the third stanza still more mournful tones, with slow time.

THE LIGHTS OF LONDON TOWN.—SIMS.

The way was long and weary,
 But gallantly they strode—

A country lad and lassie—
   Along the heavy road.
The night was dark and stormy,
   But blithe of heart were they,
For shining in the distance
   The lights of London lay.
O gleaming lamps of London, that gem the
     city's crown,
   What fortunes lie within you,
O Lights of London Town.

The years passed on and found them
   Within the mighty fold,
The years had brought them trouble,
   But brought them little gold.
Oft from their garret window,
   On long, still summer nights,
They'd seek the far-off country
   Beyond the London lights.
O mocking lamps of London, what weary eyes
     look down
   And mourn the day they saw you,
O Lights of London Town.

With faces worn and weary,
   That told of sorrow's load,
One day a man and woman
   Crept down a country road.

They sought their native village
  Heart-broken from the fray;
Yet shining still behind them
  The Lights of London lay.
O cruel lamps of London, if tears your light
     could drown,
  Your victims' eyes would weep them,
O Lights of London Town.

THE WHISPER.

[NOTE.—The *whisper* is but little used in recitation; tho "half-whisper" is substituted, as very few can give a whisper so as to be understood at a distance. We give the exercise to strengthen the organs of speech.]

Tho practice of reading or reciting in a whisper so as to be understood in every part of a large room strengthens the organs of speech by bringing them more powerfully into play.

Whispering in this manner is also beneficial to the lungs, as it demands the full expansion of the chest, a deep inspiration, a powerful expulsion of the breath, and the practice of frequent pausing and renewing the supply of breath, without which a forcible whisper cannot be sustained.

Exercise.

Give "The Bread of St. Jodokus" in "The Whisper."

THE BREAD OF ST. JODOKUS.

'To prove how pure a heart his servant bore,
One day the Lord to St. Jodokus' door
Came begging bread in garments worn and poor.

"Good steward," spake Jodokus, "give him
    bread."
"One loaf alone remains," the steward said,
"For thee and me, the faithful dog beside."
"Give!" said the saint; "will not the Lord
    provide?"

The steward marked the single loaf with care,
And cut four pieces, each an equal share.
Then to the beggar, in no friendly tone:
"One each for thee and me, the abbot one,
One for the dog, since I can but obey."
Jodokus smiled; the beggar went his way.

Not long, and in yet wretcheder disguise,
Once more the Lord asked bread with pleading
    eyes.
"Give him my piece," Jodokus gently said;
"The Lord provides." The steward gave the
    bread.

Again the Lord beside the threshold stood,
And, faint with hunger, begged a little food.
" Give him thy portion," thus Jodokus said;
" The Lord provides." The steward gave the
    bread.

A little while, and naked, blind, and lame,
The fourth time came the Lord, and begged
    the same.
" Give the dog's piece," the holy man replied;
" The Lord who feeds the ravens will provide."

The steward gave. The beggar left the gate,
And a voice cried aloud, " Thy faith is great!
Thy Lord hath proved His servant's loyalty—
As thou hast trusted, be it done to thee! "

The steward looked, and in the tranquil bay,
Behold! four laden ships at anchor lay.
Far up their sides the water's dimpling line
Broke round their holds well stored with bread
    and wine.

Joyful the steward hastened to the strand,
And saw no man upon the vessel stand;
But on the shore a snow-white banner waved,
Whereon in golden lines these words were
    graved:

" Four ships He sends who doth the ravens feed,
To him who hath four times supplied His need.

One for the abbot, thus the lists begin;
The steward and the dog like portions win,
The fourth is for the sender's needy kin!"

SUSPENSIVE QUANTITY.

Prolonging the end of a word, without an'
actual pause, is called " suspensive quantity."

In the following example for practice it is
marked thus (—). The short pause is marked
thus (|),while longer ones are marked thus (||).

WASHINGTON.

It matters very little | what immediate spot |
may have been the birthplace of such a man
as Washington. No people | can claim || no
country | can appropriate him. The boon of
Providence to the human race | his fame | is
eternity || and his dwelling-place creation.
Though it was the defeat | of our arms | and
the disgrace | of our policy || I almost bless the
convulsion | in which he had his origin. If the
heavens thundered | and the earth rocked ||
yet | when the storm passed | how pure was the
climate | that it cleared || how bright | in the
brow of the firmament | was the planet | which
it revealed to us!

In the production of Washington | it does
really appear | as if nature | were endeavoring

to improve upon herself || and that all the vir-
tues of the ancient world | were but so many
studies | preparatory to the patriot of the new.
Individual instances | no doubt there were |
splendid exemplifications | of some single qual-
ification. Cæsar | was merciful || Scipio | was
continent || Hannibal | was patient. But | it
was reserved for Washington | to blend them
all in one || and | like the lovely masterpiece of
the Grecian artist | to exhibit | in one glow of
associated beauty | the pride of every model |
and the perfection of every master. As a
general || he marshalled the peasant | into a
veteran | and supplied by discipline | the
absence of experience. As a statesman || he
enlarged the policy of the cabinet | into the
most comprehensive system | of general ad-
vantage. And such | was the wisdom of his
views | and the philosophy of his counsels ||
that | to the soldier | and the statesman | he
almost added | the character of the sage.

A conqueror | he was untainted with the
crime of blood || a revolutionist | he was free
from any stain of treason | for aggression com-
menced the contest | and his country called
him to the field. Liberty | unsheathed his
sword || necessity | stained || victory | returned
it.

If he had paused *here* | history might have doubted | what station to assign him ‖ whether at the head of her citizens | or her soldiers ‖ her heroes | or her patriots.   But the last glorious act | *crowns* his career | and banishes all hesitation.   Who | like Washington | after having emancipated a hemisphere | resigned | its crown ‖ and preferred the retirement of domestic life | to the adoration of a land | he might almost be said to have created ?

How shall we rank thee | upon glory's page,
Thou *more* than *soldier* | and just *less* than
    sage !
All thou *hast* been | reflects less praise | on thee,
Far less | than all thou hast forborn to be.

TIME OR RATE.

Is time a property of the voice ?

Although time or duration is frequently spoken of in books of elocution as a property of the voice, it simply relates to its continnance for a longer or shorter period.

Upon what must the rate of utterance depend ?

The rate of utterance must depend upon the feeling, sentiment, or thought to be expressed.

For practice in elocution we have: quick time, very quick time, moderate time, slow time, and very slow time.

Example of Moderate and Slow Time.

(The king's part is an example of "moderate time," while the priest's rôle takes "slow time.")

—— *THE KING'S CHRISTMAS.*

With an hundred yarls at least
Held King Orm his Yule-tide feast,
    Drinking merrily;
Foamed the ale; the din of revels
Sounded down the long sand levels
    Of the wild North Sea.

Berserks chanted runes and rhymes;
Sagas of the elder times,
    Deeds of force and might,
Mixed with hymns to martyrs glorious
And the white Christ, the victorious,
    Born a babe to-night.

Midnight came, and like a spell
On the hall a silence fell—
    Hushed the Berserk's tale;
Only the deep ocean thunder,
And the pine groves rent asunder
    By the Norland gale.

In that silence of the feast
Rose a white-haired Christian priest,
    Spoke with accents mild:
" Will not each some offering proffer,
Each some birth-night present offer
    To the new-born Child ? "

Up there started Svend the bold,
Red his shaggy locks as gold,
    Black as night his eye;
" Lands of Norden fields twice twenty
Miles, where firs grow tall and plenty,
    To the Church give I."

Runald next; where sailed his crew
Sea-wolves swam and eagles flew,
    Watching for the slain.
" Gold I give—doubloons an hundred,
Last year in Sevilla plundered,
    When we ravaged Spain."

Thus they shouted, each and all,
Through the long, low-raftered hall
    Each his gift proclaimed.
Then again the hush unbroken,
For the king had not yet spoken,
    Nor his offering named.

In a sweet and gentle tone
Brave King Orm spoke from his throne:
    " What befits the king ?

Christian priest, I pray thee tell me,
That no other may excel me
   In the gift I bring."

In the silence of the feast
Spoke again the white-haired priest,
   'Mid the listening throng:
" Pardon grant, O king, and pity
To all men in field or city
   Who have done thee wrong.

" Who so pardoneth his foes
On his Lord a gift bestows
   More than lands and sea.
Such a gift—it cometh solely
From a heart that's royal wholly
   With heaven's royalty."

" Be it so," the king replied,
" All men, from this Christmas-tide,
   Brothers do I call."
Through the hall all heads bowed loyal:
" King, thy gift has proved thee royal;
   Thou surpassest all! "

That sweet Yule-tide gift went forth,
Bearing through the rugged North
   Blessings far and wide.
Men grew gentler to each other
And each called his neighbor brother
   From that Christmas-tide.

Very Slow Time.

BREAK, BREAK, BREAK.—TENNYSON.

Break, break, break,
　On thy cold gray stones, O Sea!
And I would that my tongue could utter
　The thoughts that arise in me.

O well for the fisherman's boy,
　That he shouts with his sister at play!
O well for the sailor lad,
　That he sings in his boat on the bay!

And the stately ships go on
　To their haven under the hill;
But O for the touch of a vanished hand,
　And the sound of a voice that is still!

Break, break, break,
　At the foot of thy crags, O Sea!
But the tender grace of a day that is dead
　Will never come back to me.

Quick Time.

(The second and seventh stanzas are examples of "quick time.")

LOCHINVAR.—LADY HERON'S SONG.

O, young Lochinvar is come out of the West,
Through all the wide Border his steed was the
　　best;

And save his good broadsword he weapon had
    none;
He rode all unarmed, and he rode all alone.
So faithful in love and so dauntless in war,
There never was knight like the young Loch-
    invar.

He stayed not for brake, and he stopped not
    for stone,
He swam the Esk River, where ford there was
    none;
But, ere he alighted at Netherby gate
The bride had consented—the gallant came late;
For a laggard in love and a dastard in war
Was to wed the fair Ellen of brave Lochinvar.

So boldly he entered the Netherby hall,
Among bridesmen, and kinsmen, and brothers,
    and all;
Then spoke the bride's father, his hand on his
    sword
(For the poor craven bridegroom spoke never a
    word),
" O, come ye in peace here, or come ye in war,
Or to dance at our bridal, young Lord Loch-
    invar ? "

" I long wooed your daughter—my suit you de-
    nied;

Love swells like the Solway, but ebbs like its
    tide;
And now I am come, with this lost love of mine
To lead but one measure, drink one cup of
    wine.
There be maidens in Scotland, more lovely by far,
That would gladly be bride to the young Loch-
    invar."

The bride kissed the goblet, the knight took it up;
He quaffed off the wine, and he threw down
    the cup.
She looked down to blush, and she looked up
    to sigh,
With a smile on her lips and a tear in her eye.
He took her soft hand ere her mother could
    bar,—
" Now tread we a measure !" said young Loch-
    invar.

So stately his form, and so lovely her face,
That never a hall such a galliard did grace;
While her mother did fret and her father did
    fume,
And the bridegroom stood dangling his bonnet
    and plume;
And the bride-maidens whispered, " T'were
    better by far

To have matched our fair cousin with young
  Lochinvar."

One touch to her hand, and one word in her ear,
When they reached the hall-door, and the
  charger stood near—
So light to the croup the fair lady he swung,
So light to the saddle before her he sprung !
"She is won ! we are gone, over bank, bush,
  and scaur !
They'll have fleet steeds that follow," quoth
  young Lochinvar.

There was mounting 'mong Graemes of the
  Netherby clan—
Fosters, Fenwicks, and Musgraves, they rode
  and they ran :
There was racing and chasing on Cannobie Lea;
But the lost bride of Netherby ne'er did they
  see.
So daring in love and so dauntless in war,
Have ye heard of gallant like the young Loch-
  invar ?

Very Quick Time.

(The portion of the following piece which is in *italics*
is an example of "very quick time." The verses are
taken from Tennyson's " The Princess.")

Home they brought her warrior dead:
  She nor swoon'd nor utter'd cry:

All her maidens, watching, said,
   "She must weep, or she will die."

Then they praised him, soft and low;
   Call'd him worthy to be loved,
Truest friend and noblest foe:
   Yet she neither spoke nor moved.

Stole a maiden from her place,
   Lightly to the warrior stept,
Took the face-cloth from the face—
   Yet she neither moved nor wept.

Rose a nurse of ninety years,
   Set his child upon her knee—
Like summer tempest came her tears—
   "*Sweet my child, I live for thee.*"

STRESS.

Is stress a property of the voice?

No; but, like time, always accompanying it.

Stress is the manner in which force is applied. Six sorts of stress are usually given: the radical, terminal, compound, median, thorough, and tremor.

Describe each stress and its use.

In the radical stress the force is applied at

the *beginning* of the sound, and it is used to express positive conviction.

In the terminal stress the force is at the *end,* and it is used to express scorn, defiance, and revenge.

The compound stress is simply the radical and terminal united. It is used to express a mingling of emotions.

In the median stress there is a gradual increase of force and as gradual a diminishing of it. It is used in poetic expression.

In the thorough stress the force is sustained. It is used in calling and proclaiming.

The tremor is a trembling of the voice. It is used to express extreme emotion, of whatever nature.

Exercise.

[We give the following model, used by us most successfully, and taken from Murdock's "Vocal Culture." Repeat each exercise six times in succession with constantly increasing force.]

" Radical stress,"	▷·	˙All;
" Vanishing or terminal stress,"	◁	All;
" Median stress,"	< >	All;
" Compound stress,"	▷ ◁	All;
" Thorough stress,"	=	All;
" Tremor,"	~ ~	All.

Give radical stress on the sound of *a* in the
word *all* in the following example:

▷   " Attend all! "

Give terminal stress on the word *all* in the
following example:

◁   " I said *all*—not one or two."

Give median stress on the word *all* in the
following example:

<> " Join *all* ye creatures in His praise."

Give compound stress on *all* in the following example:

▷ ◁ " What!   All ?   Did they *all* fail ?"

Give thorough stress on the word *all* in the
following example:

═══   " Come one—come all!"

Give the tremor on the word *all* in the following example:

∼∼   " Oh! I have lost you all! "

INFLECTIONS.

" Slides " or inflections are simply variations
in pitch.

The simple slides are two—the rising, marked
╱, and the falling, marked ╲.

Explain the mechanism of these slides.

" Each inflection has an opening force and

fulness, from which it tapers softly to its acute or grave termination. The more emphatic an inflection is, the lower it begins when it is called *rising,* and the higher it begins when it is named *falling.*" (Bell.)

Exercises on Rising and Falling Slides.

1.   I come to *bury* Caesar, not to *praise* him.

[The pupil must remember that an *intense rising* slide is given by taking a *lower* pitch and then rising, and an intense falling slide is executed by taking a higher pitch and then descending.]

2.   Indeed—is it?

Indeed—can it be?

Indeed—it is.

Indeed—it must be.

3. *Ham.* Will you play upon this pipe?

Guild. My lord, 1 cannot.

Ham. I pray you.

Guild. Believe me, I cannot.

Ham. I do beseech you.

Guild. I know no touch of it, my lord.

[The pupil must practise vowels, words, and phrases with rising and falling slides until he has gained control of these fundamental movements of the voice.]

In sadness, grief, or suffering the slides become semi-tonic or minor. They may be either rising or falling.

Exercise on Minor Slides.

Oh, my lord,

Must I then leáve you ? Must I needs forego

So goód, so noble, and so trúe a master ?

O savè me, Hubert, savè me! My eyes are out

Even with the fierce looks of these bloody men.

The simple slides united form the circumflexes or waves. They are named rising or falling as their termination turns upwards or downwards.

Rising circumflex, $\vee$.

Falling circumflex, $\wedge$.

The rising slides indicate doubt, indifference, appeal, or connect with what has been said.

The falling slides express certainty, completeness, and the will of the speaker.

The circumflex slides are used in irony, double meaning, and figurative language.

Exercise on Rising and Falling Circumflexes.

If you said so, then I said so. Oho! did you say so? So they shook hands and were sworn brothers.

["Delivery is a kind of music whose excellence consists in a variety of tones which rise or fall according to the things they have to express. The voice rises in doubt (′), it falls in certainty (‵), and it neither rises nor falls in hesitation (—)."—Delaumosne.]

In the following exercise the important changes of pitch or slides are marked.

MONA'S WATERS.

Oh! Mona's waters are blue and bright
    When the sun shines out like a gay young
        lovér;
But Mona's waves are dark as night
    When the face of heáven is clouded over.
The wild wind drives the crested foam
    Far up the steep and rocky mountaín,
And booming echoes drown the voíce,
    The silvery voice, of Mona's fountain.

Wild, wild against that mountain's side
    The wrathful waves were up and beatíng,
When stern Glenvarloch's chieftain came,
    With anxious brow and hurried greetíng.

He bàde the widowed mother sénd
  (While loud the tempest's voice was ragíng)
Her fair young son across the flood,
  Where winds and waves their strife were
      wagìng.

And still that fearful mother práyed,
  "Oh! yet delay, delay till mornìng,
For weak the hand that guides our bark,
  Though brave his heart, all danger scòrning."
Little did stern Glenvarloch heed:
  The safety of my fortress towér
Depends on tidings he must bring
  From Fairlee bank, within the hòur.

" See'st thou, across the sullen wave,
  A blood-red banner wildly streamìng ?
That flag a message brings to me
  Of which my foes are little dreamìng.
The boy *must* put his boat across
  (Gold shall repay his hour of dangér),
And bring me back, with care and speed,
  Three letters from the light-browed strangèr."

The orphan boy leaped lightly in;
  Bold was his eye and brow of beáuty,
And bright his smile as thus he spoke:
  " I do but pay a vassal's dùty.

Fear not for me, O mother dear!
　See how the boat the tide is spúrning;
The storm will cease, the sky will clear,
　And thou wilt watch me safe returning."

His bark shot on, now up, now down,
　Over the waves—the snowy-crestéd;
Now like a dart it sped along,
　Now like a white-winged sea-bird restèd;
And ever, when the wind sank low,
　Smote on the ear that woman's wailíng,
As long she watched, with streaming eyes,
　That fragile bark's uncertain sailing.

He reached the shore—the letters claimed;
　Triumphant, heard the stranger's wónder
That one so young should brave alone
　The heaving lake, the rolling thùnder.
And once again his snowy sail
　Was seen by her—that mourning móther;
And once she heard his shouting voice—
　That voice the waves were soon to smòther.

Wild burst the wind, wide flapped the sail,
　A crashing peal of thunder followéd;
The gust swept o'er the water's face
　And caverns in the deep lake hollowèd.

The gust swept past, the waves grew calm,
  The thunder died along the mountáin;
But where was he who used to play,
  On sunny days, by Mona's fountain?

His cold corpse floated to the shore
  Where knelt his lone and shrieking mothér;
And bitterly she wept for him,
  The widow's son who had no brothèr!
She raised his arm—the hand was closed;
  With pain his stiffened fingers párted:
And on the sand three letters dropped!—
  His last dim thought—the faithful-beàrted

Glenvarloch gazed, and on his brow
  Remorse with pain and grief seemed blend-
      íng;
A purse of gold he flung beside
  That mother, o'er her dead child bendìng.
Oh! wildly laughed that woman then,
  "Glenvarloch! would ye dare to measúre
The holy life that God has given
  Against a heap of golden treasúre?

" Ye spurned my prayer, for we were poor;
  But know, proud man, that God hath powér
To smite the king on Scotland's throne,
  The chieftain in his fortress towèr.

Frown on! frown on! I fear ye not;
  We've done the last of chieftain's bidding;
And cold he lies, for whose young sake
  I used to bear your wrathful chiding.

" Will gold bring back his cheerful voice
  That used to win my heart from sorrów ?
Will silver warm the frozen blood,
  Or make my heart less lone to-morrów ?
Go back and seek your mountain home;
  And when ye kiss your fair-haired daughtér,
Remember him who died to-night
  Beneath the waves of Mona's watèr."

Old years rolled on and new ones came—
  Foes dare not brave Glenvarloch's tówer;
But naught could bar the sickness out
  That stole within fair Annie's bowèr.
The o'erblown floweret in the sun
  Sinks languid down and withers daíly,
And so she sank—her voice grew faint,
  Her laugh no longer sounded gaíly.

Her step fell on the old oak floor
  As noiseless as the snow-shower's drifting;
And from her sweet and serious eyes
  They seldom saw the dark lid lifting.

"Bring aid! Bring aid!" the father cries;
  "Bring aid!" each vassal's voice is crying;
"The fair-haired beauty of the isles,
  Her pulse is faint—her life is flying!"

He called in vain; her dim eyes turned
  And met his own with parting sorrów,
For well she knew, that fading girl,
  That he must weep and wail the morròw.
Her faint breath ceased; the father bent
  And gazed upon his fair-haired daughtér.
What thought he on?—The widow's son,
  And the stormy night by Mona's watèr.

PROJECTION OF TONE, OR DISTANCING.

What is meant by "projection of tone," or distancing?

Throwing the voice to a distance, as one would throw a ball from the hand, is called "distancing," and is a very important part of vocal technique.

How is it accomplished?

One should open the throat and nostrils, as if about to gape. Take breath, hold it, and then throw the voice to the required distance.

Are only loud tones projected?

On the contrary, the gentlest tones may be projected—indeed, in practising "distancing" we recommend beginning with the gentlest tones.

Give the following exercise with "gentle force," but projecting the tones to a person at a distance.

EACH AND ALL.—EMERSON.

Little thinks, in the field, yon red-cloaked
    clown,
Of thee from the hill-top looking down;
The heifer that lows in the upland farm,
Far-heard, lows not thine ear to charm;
The sexton, tolling his bell at noon,
Deems not that great Napoleon
Stops his horse and lists with delight,
While his files sweep round yon Alpine height;
Nor knowest thou what argument
Thy life to thy neighbor's creed has lent.

All are needed by each one;
Nothing is fair or good alone.
I thought the sparrow's note from heaven,
Singing at dawn on the alder bough;
I brought him home, in his nest, at even;
He sings the song, but it pleases not now,
For I did not bring home the river and sky;—
He sang to my ear—they sang to my eye.

The delicate shells lay on the shore;
The bubbles of the latest wave
Fresh pearls to their enamel gave,
And the bellowing of the savage sea
Greeted their safe escape to me.

I wiped away the weeds and foam,
I fetched my sea-born treasure home;
But the poor, unsightly, noisome things
Had left their beauty on the shore
With the sun, and the sand, and the wild up-
    roar.

The lover watched his graceful maid
As 'mid the virgin train she strayed;
Nor knew her beauty's best attire
Was woven still by the snow-white choir.
At last she came to his heritage,
Like the bird from the woodlands to the cage.—
The gay enchantment was undone—
A gentle wife, but fairy none.

Then I said, " I covet truth;
Beauty is unripe childhood's cheat;
I leave it behind with the games of youth."

As I spoke, beneath my feet
The ground-pine curled its pretty wreath,
Running over the club-moss burrs;
I inhaled the violet's breath;

Around me stood the oaks and firs;
Pine-cones and acorns lay on the ground;
Over me soared the eternal sky,
Full of light and of deity.

Again I saw, again I heard
The rolling river, the morning bird—
Beauty through my senses stole;
I yielded myself to the perfect whole.

Give the same selection as if reciting it solely for the benefit of a person close beside the speaker.

[The student will thus understand the difference existing between a projected tone and one that is not projected.]

[Miss Anna Dickinson was once asked how she was able to make herself heard in every part of Music Hall, Boston, which seats nearly three thousand people.

Opposite the platform whereon stands the speaker is the figure of Apollo. It is high above the audience and at the greatest distance from the speaker. Miss Dickinson made herself audible to all in the hall by *projecting her tones* to Apollo. She herself thus describes her method of "distancing." "When I come onto the platform, and find myself facing the great audience, I make a full pause, then take a good ready, and speak to Apollo."]

GESTURE.

What is gesture?

Gesture is usually defined as the various postures and movements of the body.

Delsarte says: "Gesture is the manifestation of the being through the activities of the body."

[Delsarte's definition of gesture is the best that has yet been given.]

["Speech is inferior to gesture, because it corresponds to the phenomena of mind; gesture is the agent of the heart, it is the persuasive agent."—Delaumosne.]

Gestures either express some state of the being or refer to objects, real or imagined.

Upon what law must all laws for gesture rest?

Upon the law of correspondence. Delsarte founded his system upon this great principle, which commands that every expression of the face, movement of the body—in a word, every outward manifestation—must correspond to and be in harmony with the emotion, sentiment, or idea to be expressed.

[Shakespeare's "Suit the action to the word,

and the word to the action," commands this outward correspondence to inner conditions which Delsarte's law enforces.]

Did Delsarte give other laws for gesture?

The following six laws are attributed to Delsarte by M. l'Abbé Delaumosne in his "*Practique de l'Art Oratoire de Delsarte,*" published in Paris in 1874: Priority, Retroaction, Opposition of Agents, Unity, Stability, and Rhythm.

PRIORITY.

What does the law of priority command?

The law of priority or sequence commands that gesture precede speech, and that the gestures of the face precede all others.

Delsarte gives the law in these words: " Let your attitude, gesture, and face foretell what you would make felt."

What does the word sequence signify?

An order of succession.

What is the law of priority sometimes called?

The law of succession.

Why?

Because all emotion must be expressed by the movement of organs in obedience to the law in this way: The expression must begin at the eye, then spread over the face to the shoulder, and then over the whole body like a wave, using each articulation of the body as it moves downward.

What does this law command applied to the face?

It commands this order of succession: First the eye, second the brow, and then the nostrils and the mouth.

What does it command applied to the arm?

First the upper part of the arm, then the fore-arm, and last the hand.

RETROACTION.

What do we learn from this law?

That the speaker makes a backward or forward movement as he is passive or active.

Explain this law more fully.

When the speaker communicates his own will or power, he is agent and advances.

When he reflects he makes a backward movement.

" In the joy of seeing a friend again, as also in fright, we start back from the object loved or hated."

" The degree of reaction will be in proportion to the emotion caused by the sight of the object."

[" The passive attitude is that of energetic natures. They have something in themselves which suffices them. This is a sort of repose; it is elasticity."]

Is this law obeyed by all persons?

It is observed by all, according to their degree of cultivation or natural refinement. Delsarte says: " Motion generally has its reaction; a projected body rebounds, and it is this rebound which we call the reaction of the motion."

Rebounding bodies are agreeable to the eye. Lack of elasticity in a body is disagreeable, from the fact that, lacking suppleness, it seems as if it must, in falling, be broken, flattened, or injured; in a word, must lose something of the integrality of its form. It is therefore the reaction of a body which proves its elasticity, and which, by this very quality, gives us a sort of pleasure in witnessing a fall, which apart from this reaction could not be other than disagreeable. Therefore, *elasticity of dynamic motions is a prime necessity from the point of view of charm.* In the vulgar man there is no reaction. In the man of distinction, on the contrary, motion is of slight extent and reaction is enormous. Reaction is both slow and rapid.

OPPOSITION OF AGENTS.

Repeat this law.

" When two limbs follow the same direction

they cannot be simultaneous without an injury to the law of opposition. Therefore direct movements should be successive and opposite movements simultaneous."

[This law is sometimes called the law of equilibrium, because it commands the opposition of the agents in action, that equilibrium may result.

Charles Wesley Emerson, in his "Physical Culture," gives testimony to the worth of this law, saying: "It is manifested in every person, in the ratio of the grace of his movements. In the awkward person this law is violated, and the violation is the secret of his awkwardness."]

Is this a valuable law?

We consider it one of the most valuable of the many laws attributed to Delsarte.

[It is affirmed by Madame Arnaud that Delsarte had studied the poses of the statues of antiquity for fifteen years before he formulated this law.]

THE LAW OF UNITY.

This law relates to the number of gestures.

But one gesture is needed for one entire thought. In impersonating we would say that the number and also the kind of gestures would depend upon the character depicted. The law of unity commands a strict correspondence in this regard.

THE LAW OF STABILITY.

This law teaches that, while the speaker is under the influence of the same sentiment the same inflection and gesture must be maintained; that the prolongation of movement is one of the great sources of effect.

[Very young orators rarely observe the law of stability—hence their ineffectiveness.]

THE LAW OF RHYTHM.

Gesture is "rhythmic" through its movement, more or less slow or more or less rapid.

How does Delsarte state this law?

"The rhythm of gesture is proportional to the mass to be moved."

This law is based upon the vibration of the pendulum.

Great levers have slow movements, small agents more rapid ones. The head moves more rapidly than the torso, and the eye has great facility of motion. "In proportion to the depth and majesty of the emotion is the deliberation and slowness of the motion; and, *vice versa*, in proportion to the superficiality and explosiveness of the emotion will be the velocity of its expression in motion."

[Gesture is melodic or inflective through the richness of its forms; harmonic through the multiplicity of parts that unite simultaneously to produce it.]

DELAUMOSNE'S NINE ATTITUDES OF THE LEGS.

These attitudes should be practised well, as pupils rarely have the necessary ease in chang-

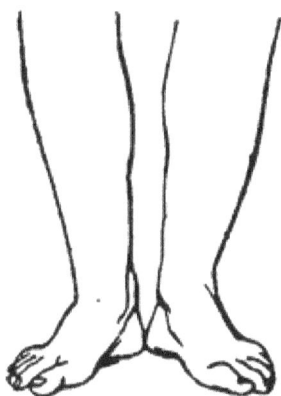

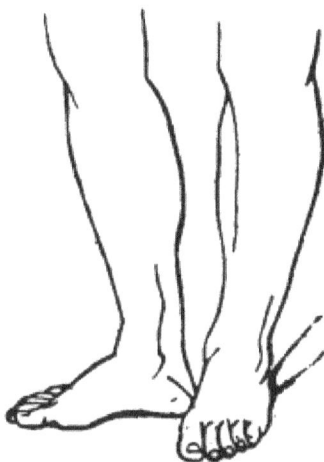

1. Respect.   2. Strength.

ing the positions of the feet; and yet upon the attitude of the legs depends the graceful expression of the rest of the form.

1. Heels nearly together, toes pointing slightly outward, with the weight of the body resting equally upon the feet. This is the attitude of respect. It characterizes old age and infancy.

2. In this attitude the *free* leg is advanced and the weight of the body rests upon the

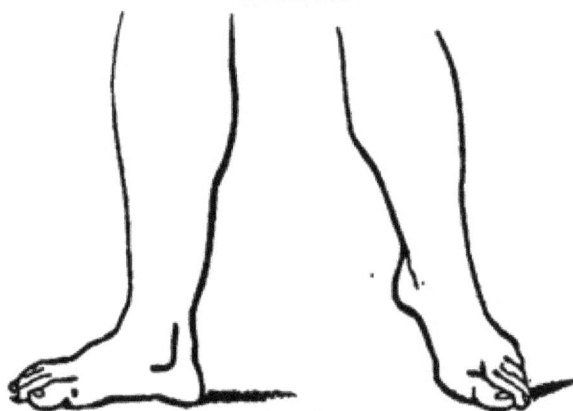

3. Vehemence.

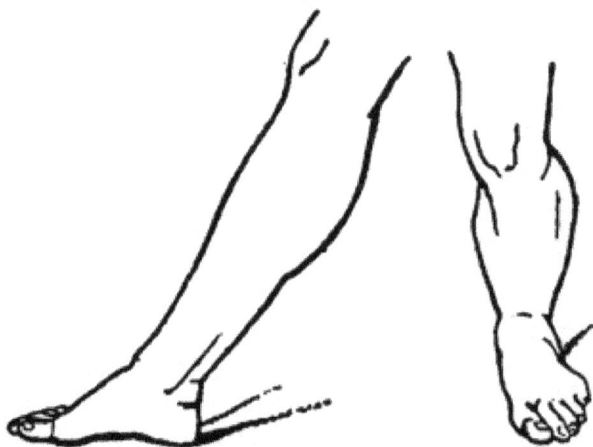

4. Weakness.

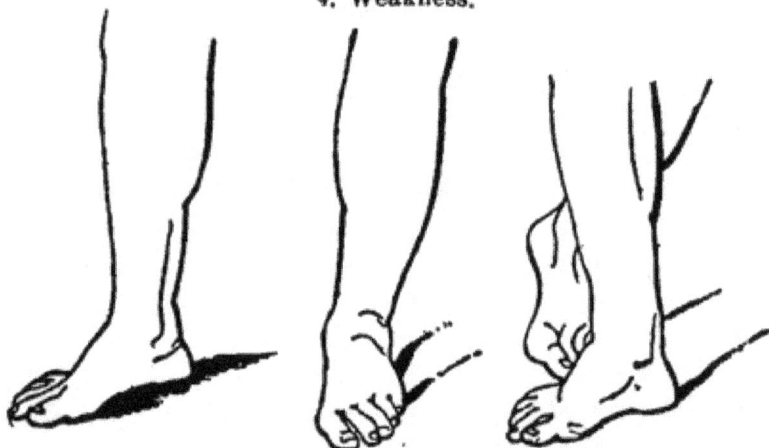

5. Passive.   6. Ceremony.

backward leg. This attitude signifies calm, strength, reflection.

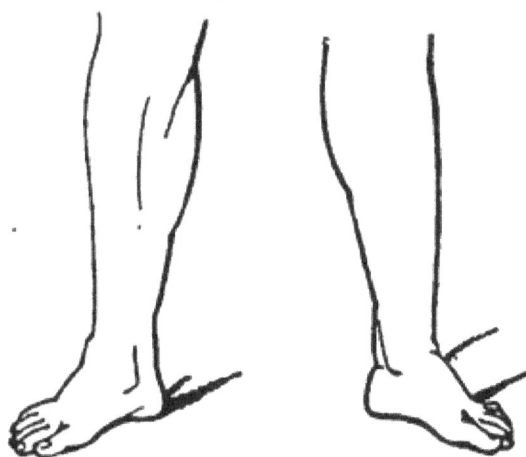

3. Here all the weight of the body is on the advanced foot. The backward leg is extended in proportion to the advancement of the torso. This attitude signifies vehemence.

7. Intoxication.

4. This attitude is assumed by carrying all the weight of the body backward and by bending the leg which bears the weight of the body. It expresses the weakness which follows vehemence. Natural weakness is expressed by the first attitude, and sudden weakness by the fourth attitude.

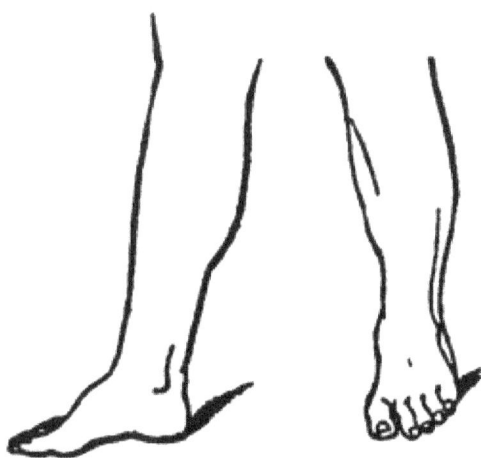

8. Hesitation.

5. This is necessitated by the inclination of the torso to one side or the other. It is a passive attitude preparatory to all oblique steps.

6. This attitude is the third, crossed. It is an attitude of great respect and ceremony, and is used only in the presence of princes.

7. Here the

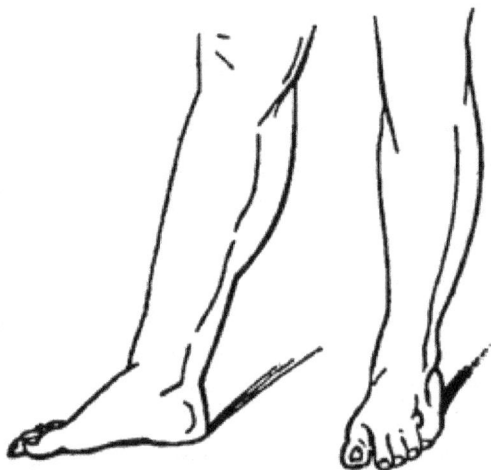

9. Defiance.

weight of the body is distributed *equally* upon the feet, which are wide apart. It is the sign of vulgar confidence, of drunkenness, and of the weak who wish to appear strong.

8. The eighth attitude is the second, with the feet farther apart. It is the sign of hesitation. The weight of the body rests equally upon the feet.

9. This attitude is an extended second. The principal weight is on the backward leg. It expresses defiance.

THE TORSO.

The torso or trunk is divided into three general divisions. The chest or upper portion corresponds to grand emotions; the middle, to the affections, and the abdominal region, to the animal propensities. Gestures directed to or from the chest express the higher emotions, such as love of God, honor, hope, etc.; those from the middle of the torso, earthly affections; and those from the abdominal region, animal propensities. The last are vulgar, and, therefore, to be avoided.

The torso expands, contracts, or relaxes in correspondence with the emotion one is depicting.

The leaning of the torso to or from an object expresses attraction or repulsion.

What portion of the torso should be most prominent in our bearing?

The upper portion of the torso, being the nobler, should be most prominent in our bearing.

How should the shoulders be held?

If the chest be held high, the shoulders will naturally fall backward and downward. "Take care of the chest and the shoulders will take care of themselves."

[All the best Greek statues present the human form standing with the chest on a vertical line with the toe.]

THE HAND.

[Delsarte was the first to apply the three kinds of motion—centrifugal, centripetal, and centred

—to human expression. To express these three kinds of motion, he invented the terms *excentric, concentric,* and *normal.*

By excentric, he means motions *from* the centre; by concentric, motions *to* the centre; and by normal, motions held in poise or balance.]

The hands when they open without effort are said to be in the normal state.

When they close they are concentric.

When they open with force they present the excentric state.

["Every one knows that with the hands we can demand or promise, call, dismiss, threaten, supplicate, ask, deny, show joy, sorrow, detestation, fear, confession, penitence, admonition, respect, and many other things now in common use."—Sheridan.]

Next to the face the hand is the most expressive of the agents.

The hand has three presentations:

The palm prone, supine, and vertical.

"The natural language of the prone palm is repression; of the supine, releasing or giving; of the vertical, repelling."

The hands applied—that is, the palms together—express the prayer of innocence.

The clasped hands are employed to supplicate; they are also used to express distress.

The folded hands—that is, the fingers of the right hand laid between the thumb and forefinger of the left, the right thumb crossing the left—express humility, dolor, and prayer.

DELAUMOSNE'S NINE ATTITUDES OF THE HAND.

1. This is the normal hand. It signifies repose, indifference.

2. This is the first attitude, with the fingers slightly extended. It signifies warmth, expansion.

3. In this attitude the hand is completely relaxed. The fingers hang lifeless, thumb falls in toward palm. It signifies prostration.

4. In this attitude the fingers close with the thumb resting on the index finger. It signifies calm, power, possession.

5. In this attitude the fingers are closed, the thumb outside the index and middle fingers. It signifies conflict.

6. In this attitude the fingers are bent, at the first joint, toward the palm. It signifies convulsion.

7. In this attitude the fingers are expanded, but not excessively. It signifies exaltation.

8. In this attitude the fingers are bent toward the palm, but separated as much as possible. It signifies execration.

6. Convulsion.

4. Power.

5. Conflict.

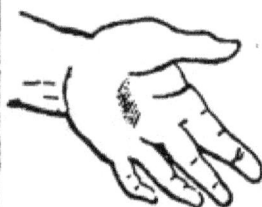

2. Expansion.

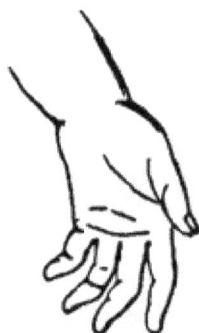

1. Indifference.

3. Prostration.

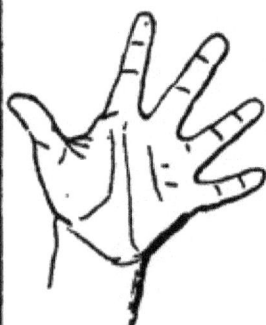

9. Exasperation.

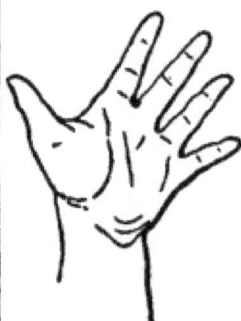

7. Exaltation.

8. Execration.

9. In this attitude the hand is open to its full extent, with the fingers as far apart as possible. It signifies exasperation.

THE ELBOW.

The elbow turned outward indicates strength, audacity, arrogance, abruptness. The elbow turned inward indicates impotence, constraint, subordination, weakness.

The elbow in poise or normal indicates ease, self-possession, calmness, an equable temper.

THE SHOULDER.

Delsarte affirmed the shoulder to be the thermometer of the sensitive and passional life. " If a man's shoulders are raised very decidedly, we know that he is decidedly impressed."

Every agreeable or painful emotion is expressed by an elevation of the shoulders. The face will tell whether the impression be joyous or sorrowful.

How many things may be said or insinuated by a shrug of the shoulders!

THE ARMS.

The arms hanging easily from the shoulder signify calm repose. Arms folded easily above the belt line express power.

The arm raised above the head with *back* of the hand exposed signifies supreme power.

Arms extended sidewise, with palms toward the audience, express welcome. The arms hanging in a lifeless manner express depression, dejection.

THE HEAD.

The upper part of the head corresponds to the upper part of the torso, and expresses the noble emotions, but in a higher degree. The eye leads in expression, in so much as it indicates objects. "The upper part of the face down to the root of the nose is the seat of thought; it is the region where our projects and resolutions are formed. It is the office of the middle and lower parts to unfold them."—(Brown.)

NINE ATTITUDES OF THE HEAD.

1. The head held easily erect signifies calm repose. It is a colorless attitude.

2. The head lifted signifies vehemence.

3. The head bowed, concentration of mind; reflection.

4. The head advanced, interest, curiosity, eagerness.

5. The head leaning toward an object expresses tenderness.

The head drawn back from an object expresses dislike.

6. The head slightly bowed directly before an object, with the eyes upon it, expresses scrutiny.

7. The head advanced toward a person or object and bowed signifies trust, veneration.

8. The head bowed and drawn back from an object which the eyes gaze upon expresses suspicious scrutiny.

9. The head lifted, with face turned upward, signifies exaltation.

Negation is expressed by a lateral movement of the head from side to side. This movement of the head also expresses sadness.

Affirmation and assent bend the head forward.

THE EYES AND EYEBROWS.

Description of Delaumosne's Chart.

1. This is the normal eye, and is colorless in expression.

2. This is the eye normal—that is, opened naturally—with the eyebrow raised. It expresses disdain.

3. This is the eye nearly open, with eyebrow drawn into a frown. It expresses ill humor.

4. The eye wide open, with the eyebrow normal, expresses stupor.

6. Firmness.

3. Ill-humor.

9. Contention of mind.

4. Stupor.

1. Normal.

7. Fatigue.

5. Astonishment.

2. Disdain.

8. Contempt.

5. The eye wide open, with the eyebrow raised, expresses astonishment.

6. The eye open, with the eyebrow lowered, expresses will-power, firmness.

7. The eye partly closed, with the eyebrow normal, expresses sleep, fatigue.

8. The eye nearly closed, with the eyebrow raised, expresses contempt.

9. The eye partly closed, with the eyebrow lowered, expresses contention of mind, a seeking for something one does not find.

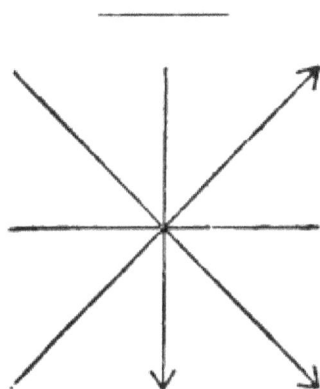

The above diagram of Delaumosne's represents the significance of the direct and oblique lines of gesture.

Gestures made by the hand and arm which follow the vertical line express affirmation. They are gestures of assent, acceptance, agreement, certainty.

Gestures which follow the horizontal line express negation. They are gestures of denial, non-agreement, opposition.

Gestures which follow the oblique line upwards and outwards express rejection of things which one contemns—light and trivial things.

Gestures which trace the oblique line downwards and outwards express rejection of things which oppress.

TECHNIQUE OF GESTURE.

Every gesture has direction, place, and extension.

Direction.—There are five points of direction: Horizontal, ascending, zenith, descending, and nadir.

Place.—There are five points of place: Front, oblique, lateral, oblique backwards, and backwards.

Extension signifies those movements of the hand by which the outline, form, action, or some other property of the object is indicated.

["It is impossible to give free play in all directions to the hand and arm without producing a series of curved lines. The widest and freest sweep of the instrument describes arcs of circles, and these arcs described by both arms project the figure of a globe."—Brown.]

Exercises.

Raise the right arm and point to the zenith
with the forefinger.

[What is the zenith?

That point in the visible celestial hemisphere
which is vertical to the spectator—the point of
the heavens directly overhead.]

Sweep the arm through 180° to the nadir.

[What is the nadir?

That point directly opposite the zenith—the
point of the celestial sphere directly under the
place where we stand.]

Same action with left arm from zenith to nadir.

The pupil now will have traced the circle of
a globe. Imagine this globe divided into upper
and lower hemispheres, as by an equator. In
technique all gestures above this horizontal line
are called *ascending* and all below it are named
descending. The pupil will now imagine two
vertical *front* lines, one a trifle to the right of
the centre of the circle and the other a trifle
to the left. Half-way from the centre (midway between the chest and shoulder) are the
oblique lines, which are forty-five degrees to the
right and left of the centre; and forty-five degrees
to the right and left of these are the *lateral*
lines; and back of these, the same distance apart,
are the *oblique backwards* and *backwards.*

For the convenience of the pupil, we give a plan of notation similar to that used in "Austin's Chironomia."

d. f., descending front.

d. o., descending oblique.

d. l., descending lateral.

d. o. b., descending oblique backwards.

h. f., horizontal front.

h. o., horizontal oblique.

h. l., horizontal lateral.

h. o. b., horizontal oblique backwards.

a. f., ascending front.

a. o.. ascending oblique.

a. l., ascending lateral.

a. o. b., ascending oblique backwards.

r. h., right hand.

l. h., left hand.

b. h., both hands.

s., supine.

p., prone.

v., vertical.

i. or ind., index finger.

upl., uplifted.

par., parallel.

cli., clinched.

cla., clasped.

ap., applied.

fol., folded.

cro., crossed.

prep., preparation.

rep., repeat.

imp., impulse.

sus., sustained.

tr., tremor.

In notating gestures the s. may be omitted from the supine hand, and r. h. from gestures to be made with the right hand singly. When the position of the hand is not notated, it is understood to be supine; and when it is not notated whether one or both hands are to be used, the right hand is understood.

MR. AUSTIN'S CLASSIFICATION OF GESTURE.

The style of gesture used must correspond to the style of the composition one is rendering.

Mr. Austin classes gestures as epic, rhetorical, and colloquial.

What styles of compositions require epic gesture?

Tragedy, epic poetry, lyric odes, and sublime description.

What are the qualities of epic gesture?

Magnificence, boldness, energy, variety, simplicity, grace, propriety, and precision.

Describe each of these qualities.

Magnificence of gesture consists in the ample

space through which the arm and hand are made to move.

Boldness consists in that elevated courage and self-confidence which ventures to hazard any action productive of a grand and striking effect. (In this sort of gesture unexpected positions, elevations, and transitions, surprise at once by their novelty and grace, and thus illustrate or enforce ideas with irresistible effect.)

Energy consists in the firmness and decision of the whole action, and in the support which the voice receives from the precision of the stroke of the gesture.

Variety consists in the ability of readily adapting suitable gestures to each sentiment, so as to avoid recurring too frequently to favorite gestures.

Simplicity consists in using such gestures as appear the natural result of the situation and sentiments.

Grace of gesture consists in the union of precision, ease, and harmony.

Propriety consists in a judicious use of those movements which are best suited to the sentiment.

Precision of gesture arises from the just preparation, the due force, and the correct timing of the action. The preparation is neither too much abridged nor too pompously displayed. The stroke is made with that degree of force which suits the character of the sentiment and speaker, and occurs on the precise syllable to be enforced. Precision gives the same effect to action that neatness of articulation gives to speech.

What are the qualities of rhetorical gesture?

Energy, variety, simplicity, and precision. Boldness and magnificence may sometimes have place.

What are the qualities of colloquial gesture?

Colloquial gestures principally require simplicity and grace. In colloquial gesture the movements are shorter and less flowing, and the action is less frequent.

Exercises on Gesture.

1. Bring right arm up until the index finger of right hand almost touches the left shoulder, palm downwards. Now sweep arm outward (the side of hand cleaving the air) until the fingers point horizontal oblique.

[Indication with the hand *prone* is used to point out objects at a distance, or, if the object be near, to express power, command, displeasure.

The pupil will be careful to observe the following order in the making of these full-arm movements. First, the upper arm; second, the forearm; finally, the hand and fingers.]

Same with the left hand, viz.: Place index finger almost upon right shoulder, then sweep arm outward to left until the index finger points horizontal left oblique. Release force, first from hand, then from forearm, and last from upper arm, and, the energy having been withdrawn, the arm will return gracefully to its place.

These movements may be practised at different altitudes.

2. Cross hands in front of chest, palms downward, then sweep arms outward until the index finger of the right hand points "right horizontal lateral," and the index finger of the left hand points "left horizontal lateral." With the index finger of the right hand trace the figure eight (8), commencing at the top of the figure.

Same exercise with the left hand.

[The pupil will remember that when the arms are inactive there is an opposition of head and torso, but when the arm is used the opposition is between the head and arm, while the torso leans from the leg which bears the weight of the body.]

RELAXATION.

[Relaxation is simply either preparation for
, action or rest after effort.

" Dynamic wealth depends upon the number of articulations brought into play."—Delsarte.]

If the student is not able to *relax* at will, or should the articulations of the body be stiff, it would be well for him to practise the following exercises.

Exercise for the Head.

Drop the head upon the chest, then, by an inclination of the torso, send it to the left, then backward, round to right shoulder, and back to chest again.

Exercise for the Arms.

Lift the forearm a little above the belt line in front, and, letting the hand and fingers hang in a relaxed and lifeless manner, move the arm up and down. The arm will shake the hand and fingers.

Same exercise, moving the forearm from right to left.

With the hand still relaxed, circle the forearm, the elbow being the centre of motion. Stretch the entire arm front, letting the hand hang lifeless, and move the arm, without bending the elbow, up and down. Practise first with right arm, then with left, then with both arms. Allow the arms to hang relaxed. Turn the torso to right and left, slinging the arms by this motion.'

Exercise for the Legs.

Stand upon a stool and allow the leg to hang relaxed from the hip; shake it by swaying the body. Practise first right leg and then left.

Opposition Movements.

Rotate the torso, at the waist line, to the right, while turning the head to the left.

Turn torso as much as possible to the left while the head turns as much as possible to the right.

Raise both arms high above the head while the head sinks upon the chest. Raise the head to normal position while the arms fall in opposition.

Advance right leg, and at the same time advance left arm. Advance right arm and left leg simultaneously.

Kneel on right knee while raising left arm toward heaven.

Kneel on left knee while raising right arm toward heaven.

Cross hands upon chest, at the same time bowing head. Extend arms, palms outward, and simultaneously raise head, clasp hands, and raise them to chest, bowing the head toward them.

Bring right hand up to chest, extend hand, palm up as if to take some object. This gesture may be used for ideas as well as objects. It signifies appeal.

In these sorts of movements the head acts in opposition. (But the pupil must remember that the movement of the head is very slight compared with that of the arm, as the arc in which the head moves is so much smaller.) The direction of the gesture of appeal will depend upon the location of the object asked for, or the position of the person appealed to. Make a gesture of appeal oblique ascending—descending—with right hand—with left hand—with both hands.

Parallel Movements.

Extend both arms horizontal front, move both to the right, the right hand leading; reverse this movement. Move both arms left, left hand leading.

Let the pupil imagine a person in front to whom the speaker wishes to show an object situated on the "right oblique ascending." The head will first turn front, then toward the object, as the arm folds toward chest of speaker in preparation for gesture. Now, as the head turns back to person front, the arm moves outward and shows object.

"Parallel movements must be successive, opposite gestures simultaneous."

WALKING.

To walk well the whole form should be well poisęd.

The head should be erect, with the chin well drawn in, the chest active, and the legs swung from the hip-joints.

In slow walking the ball of the foot touches the ground first.

Ordinarily, however, the heel strikes the ground a trifle before the ball of the foot.

THE PIVOT.

When one wishes to turn in walking "the pivot" should be employed.

To turn to the left, advance the right foot, transfer the weight to it, and, resting the ball of the left foot very lightly on the floor, pivot to the left. Both heels should just clear the floor.

To turn to the right, advance the left foot, and then transfer the weight of the body to it, maintaining the balance of the body by resting lightly on the ball of the right foot, pivot to the right, the heels of both feet just clearing the floor.

BOWING.

The bow is a slight inclination of the body, beginning with the head and passing over the entire form. The courtesy, which is still used in the presence of persons of rank, is made by placing one foot behind and slowly bending the backward knee, the other knee also bending. Rise slowly to an erect position and draw the forward foot back. Do not bring the backward one forward, as it bears the principal weight of the body; also because using first one leg and then the other is more harmonious. Grace is born of contrast.

These remarks apply only to the bow made by females.

The attitude of respect is the one assumed by a boy when about to bow. The heels are nearly together and the toes pointed slightly outward. The head bends, and the torso is also slightly inclined; the torso first returns to an erect position, and the head follows.

[Some persons make three bows—one front, one to the right, and one to the left. However, the method to be preferred is to glance over the entire audience and make but one.]

KNEELING.

Place one foot behind and bend the knee until it rests upon the ground. In kneeling upon a stage or platform the speaker should sink upon the knee next to the audience. For example, if upon the right side of the platform the right knee is the one to rest upon; and if upon the left side, the left knee should be brought to the ground. In sinking to the ground incline the torso forward and the head backward.

HOW TO SIT.

To take a seat with grace, one foot should be placed behind, as if about to courtesy; carry the weight of the body to it, and, as the weight of the body is transferred to it, bend the torso forward and the head backward. Be careful not to "flop" or "drop" into the seat, but have the feet bear the weight of the body until the seat is reached.

SPEECH.

Upon what does perfection of speech depend?

Primarily upon a correct production of syllables and elementary sounds. Speech is correctly defined as the faculty of expressing thought by articulate sounds.

["All human utterances may be resolved into elementary sounds or *oral actions;* and all the varieties of phonic elements in different languages are the result of definite mechanical adjustments of the organs of speech. The organs are the same in all men; and consequently every person possesses naturally the ability to speak any or every language."—Bell.]

Name the operative vocal organs and their office.

The operative vocal organs are: the lungs, to supply breath; the glottis, to vocalize it; the pharynx, to compress it; the tongue and the lips, to parcel it.

What of the teeth?

They are not operative in speech. In mastication they are so. In speech we have simply to keep them out of the way.

["Notwithstanding the fact that grammarians have used the term 'dentals' to denote a whole class of elementary sounds, there is not an element that cannot be distinctly formed by a speaker who has not a tooth in his head. The sound of *th* is the one in which the teeth are the most obviously employed; but the characteristic quality of the *th* may be produced with the tip of the tongue to any accessible part of the mouth—to the palate, to the gum, to the teeth, or even to the lips."—Bell.]

After the correct production of the sound of a word, what is next in importance?

The proper placing of the accent. Accent is the greater stress which is given to a syllable. By changing the accent we often change the meaning. (Examples: Ac'cent, a noun; accent', a verb. Pres'ent, a noun; present', a verb.)

In words of three or more syllables there are secondary accents employed.

[The pupil should make lists of words, marking primary and secondary accents.]

What is emphasis?

Emphasis is the greater prominence we give to a word or phrase.

Emphasis is to the word what accent is to the syllable.

Where should emphasis be placed?

Wherever the "point" of the sentence lies. A clear conception of the author's meaning is absolutely necessary before one can give it to another, through correct accentuation.

[In the examples for practice the emphatic words are printed in *italics*.]

Exercise.

I gave him those keys.
I *gave* him those keys.
I gave *him* those keys.
I gave him *those* keys.

Exercise.

At the close of the *day*—when the hamlet is still,
 And mortals the sweets of *forgetfulness* prove;
When naught but the *torrent* is heard on the hill,
 And naught but the *nightingale's* song in
 the grove:
It was *thus,* by *the cave of the mountain* afar,
 While his *harp* rung symphonious, a *hermit*
 began;
No *more* with himself or with *nature* at *war,*
 He thought as a *sage,* tho' he felt as a *man.*

GROUPING.

Grouping or phrasing is effected by a pause.

When two or more words are used substantively, pronominally, adjectively, or adverbially they should be uttered as one.

Law. " No two words should be united which have not a mutual relation in forming sense; and no two such words should be separated."

Examples.

[The hyphens indicate that the words they are placed between are to be read as one reads compound words.]

Smith | the - brother - in - law - of - Adams | the - tailor | came | as - soon - as - he - heard | the - terrible - news.

William | so - great - was - his - interest - in-
the - case | returned | to - the - city | on - the -
first | train | that left | after - he - had - fin-
ished | his - necessary - business.

This separating words into groups to express
ideas is a most important part of elocution. It
should be impressed upon the youngest student
that *each word is not the sign of an idea*—and
that grammatical words are rather to be considered merely as the syllables of what has been
called the " oratorical word," which fully expresses the idea, or completes some part of it.

TRANSITION.

The speaker must seize every opportunity for
change in *Quality, Force, Pitch,* and *Time*
which the recitation presents.

The ability to pass, with ease, from grave to
gay, from lively to severe, is, in most instances,
the result of discipline.

The following exercise will give the pupil
opportunity to practise "transition."

CARACTACUS.

Oro-
tund.
Close your gates, O priests of Janus!
close your brazen temple gates!
For the bold Ostorius Scapula invokes
the peaceful fates;

And the brave·Britannic legion at the
Arch of Triumph waits.

Pure
tone.

Bold Ostorius—home returning—for the
island war is o'er;
And the wild Silurian rebels shall arise
in arms no more:
Captive stands their savage monarch on
the Tiber's golden shore.

Gradu-
ally in-
crease
volume
of
voice.

Crowded are the banks of Tiber, crowded
is the Appian way;
And through all the Via Sacra ye may
mark the dense array
Of the tramping throngs who celebrate
a Roman gala-day.

Caractacus! Caractacus! Oh! full many
a Roman child

Quick
time.

To its mother's breast at midnight has
been caught in terror wild,

Aspi-
rated.

When some fearful dream of Britain's
chief her sleeping sense beguiled.

Thrice in battle sank our Eagles—shame
that Romans lived to tell!

Moder-
ate
force.

Thrice three years our baffled legions
strove this rebel chief to quell:
Vain were all our arms against him, till
by treachery he fell.

Now, behold, he is our captive! in the
    market-place he stands,
And around him are the lictors and the
    stern Pretorian bands—
Stands he like a *king* among them, lift-
    ing high his shackled hands.

Sure he sees the steel-clad cohorts, and
    he marks the lictors nigh,
Yet he stands before the monarch with
    a glance as proudly high
As if *he*, in truth, were Cæsar, and
    'twere Claudius that should die.

Gradually increase force.

Gazes he o'er prince and people, with a
    glance of wondering light,—
O'er the Rostra, o'er the Forum, up the
    Palatinian height,
O'er the serried ranks of soldiers
    stretching far beneath his sight.

Tramping onward move the legions,
    tramping on with iron tread,
While Ostorius, marching vanward,
    proudly bends his martial head—
Proudly bends to the ovation, meed of
    those whom valor led.

Gradually louder.

Statue-like, in savage grandeur, stands
    the chief of Britain's isle;

Monotone.

And his bearded lip is wreathing, as
   with silent scorn, the while.

Ener-
getic
force.
  "Bold barbarian! dost thou mock us,
    mock us with that bitter smile?

Oro-
tund.
  "Lo! thou standest in the Forum,
    where the stranger's voice is free,
Where the captive may bear witness—
   thus our Roman laws decree!
Lift thy voice, O chief of Britons!
   'Tis the Cæsar speaks to thee!

  "Lift thy voice, O wondering stranger!
Increase
the vol-
ume of
tone.
    thou hast marked our Roman state;
All the terrors, all the glories, that on
    boundless empire wait!
Boldly speak thy thought, O Briton, be
   it framed in love or hate!"

Thus our monarch to the stranger.
   Then, from off his forehead fair,
Backward, with a Jove-like motion,
   flung the chief his golden hair:
Soft
oro-
tund.
And he said, "O king of Romans!
    freely I my thought declare.

  "Vanquished is my warlike nation,
    stricken by the Roman sword;
Slow
and
sad.
Lost to me my wife and children, long
    have I their fate deplored;

They are gone—but gloomy Hertha still
enthralls their hapless lord.

Gradu-
ally
louder.
" Yet I murmur not, but *wonder*—wonder, as in Jotna dreams,
At each strange and glittering marvel
that before my vision gleams;
At the blaze of Roman glory which
upon my senses streams.

Oro-
tund.
Pure
tone.
"Romans! even as gods ye prosper,
boundless are your gifts and powers!
Ye have fields with grain o'erladen,
gardens thick with fruits and flowers,
Louder.
Halls of shining marble builded, cities
strong with battling towers.

" I have marked your gorgeous dwellings
and your works of wondrous art:
Bridges high in air suspended, columned
shrine, and gilded mart,
Median
stress.
And I marvelled—much I marvelled—in
my poor barbarian heart.

Oro-
tund.
" For this day I saw your mighty gods
beneath the Pantheon dome,—
Gods of gold, and bronze, and silver,—
and I marvelled, king of Rome,
Gentle
force.
That such wealthy gods should envy
me my poor, barbarian home!"

Ceased the chief, and on the pavement
    sadly sank his tearful eyes,
And the wondering crowds around him
    held their breath in mute surprise;
Held their breath—and then outburst-
    ing, clove the air with sudden cries:

Thor-
ough
stress.
    " Cæsar, he hath spoken bravely! Clau-
        dius, he hath spoken well! "
Not unmoved the brow of Cæsar—it
    hath lost the Claudian frown;

Slow.
And a tear upon his royal cheek is
    slowly trickling down:
Never purer gem than Pity's tear en-
    riched a monarch's crown!

Yet he speaks in anger's accents: " Ho!
    advance the fasces now;
Loud.
Lictors! close ye round the scorner!
    Ha! barbarian, smilest thou ?
There is one beneath whose glances
    even thy haughty soul shall bow!"

Thus spoke Claudius, and the soldiers,
    opening round the curule chair,
Half revealed a form majestic mid the
    lictors bending there,—
Half revealed a stately woman, mantled
    by her radiant hair.

Quick.   Flashed the captive's eye with sunlight;
    burned his cheek with new-born life—
    Hope, and fear, and doubt, and glad-
    ness, held by turns their eager strife—
    Then two hearts and voices mingled,
    murmuring, " Husband! " answering
    " Wife! "

[In the last stanza the reciter must picture, by " the shade," *hope, fear, doubt,* and *gladness.* The word " husband! " should be given in a sweet tremulous tone, and the word " wife! " in a *full tone,* replete with love and gladness.]

PICTURING.

What is picturing?

Picturing in elocution consists in painting vividly the scenes and characters to be portrayed. Picturing is, therefore, a summary of the art of elocution. To picture well, one must, first of all, have a clear conception of the scene; second, one must locate objects in an artistic manner, introduce the different characters of the piece by looks and gesture; and finally, one must study each rôle and represent the character truthfully. This implies a vast amount of labor; but each recitation given in *this* manner is a work of art, and is an illustration of the application of the laws and principles of expression.

HYGIENE.

By Charles V. Burke, M.D.,

Clinical Physician and Asst.-Pathologist to St. Michael's Hospital, Newark, N. J.

INTRODUCTION.

In the following pages it has been my endeavor to give an outline of the preventive value of exercise, especially of respiratory exercise, and to direct attention to a few important points in the hygiene of school life.

It is a mistake to think that only those who have "talent" should receive elocutionary instruction, and the ability to "speak a piece" is the least of the benefits derived from such instruction. The education of the vocal apparatus involves a development which not only adds an accomplishment, but is a real preventive of disease. If a course in elocution resulted only in the student's learning how to breathe properly, he would be amply repaid.

The need of some knowledge of the right use of the body is fast becoming recognized by teachers, and it is to be hoped that a course in elementary physiology and hygiene will soon have a place in every school curriculum.

Teachers are requested to consult works upon these subjects, and students should be encouraged to pursue further a study which can only redound in good to the individual and the community.

As this is written for those who have no, or but slight knowledge of such matters, I have avoided technical terms as far as possible, and have tried to present a few fundamental ideas in an easily assimilable form.

PREVENTIVE VALUE OF ELOCU-TIONARY EXERCISE.

In all times it has been recognized that some individuals were susceptible to certain morbid influences and that others were not. When a person is susceptible to invasion by a disease he is said to have a predisposition to that disease. Such a predisposition may be either hereditary or acquired.

We cannot enter into the consideration of the mysteries of heredity, but suffice it to say that it is undeniable that a man's progenitors may bequeath him a body peculiarly susceptible to the diseases from which they suffered. Acquired predisposition is a more tangible thing, and it is to this we will direct our attention.

Every living body is constantly fighting disease. The excitants of disease are continually entering the body by every channel, and are as continually being destroyed or rendered innocuous. The body resists disease. This resistance to morbid influences rises and falls with the vital tone of the tissues. Anything that lessens the vitality of the tissues lessens resistance. Thus, pre-existing disease, malnutrition from any cause, paves the way for the ubiquitous germ, offers a favorable soil for its growth and multiplication, and opens the door which in health was closed and guarded.

Modern scientists have demonstrated that many diseases are caused by certain low forms of plant life, bacteria. Bacteria exist everywhere, and if all forms were pathogenic (disease producing) mankind would soon be annihilated. But such is, happily, not the case. Many species are harmless to man, others are even beneficial; the alimentary canal swarms with bacteria which aid in carrying on certain food changes. The micro-organism which interests us chiefly in this chapter is called the tubercle bacillus. It is the active agent in the production of that dreaded disease, tuberculosis of the lungs—consumption. One has but to read a few of the weekly mortality reports published in the newspapers to learn of the part played for the Reaper by this disease, and to appreciate the importance of anything that would tend to lessen the suffering and death laid to its account. Hundreds of its victims, in all but the final stages, move among us, and through that filthy habit of promiscuous expectoration deposit in the streets, in public buildings, in vehicles, everywhere, myriads of virulent germs. These dry, and the wind blows them, still living, in our faces, into our mouths and noses, and we breathe them into our lungs, and we swallow them. Follow these germs into the lungs of a person who has breathed improperly for years. There is a portion of his lung, generally at the apex, which has been seldom fully aerated; its circulation is sluggish, its nutrition is poor, its vitality is lowered. Here the bacilli find a fertile soil; they multiply and produce their characteristic manifestations. The person is now a consumptive, and if prompt and intelligent treatment does not change the conditions, he slowly but surely sinks to his death.

It is important that everybody should know something of the cause and mode of spread of tuberculosis, for it is the most widespread and fatal of all the diseases that we have to battle against, and because it is a distinctly preventable disease.

Aside from sanitary measures in the isolation of the sick and the destruction of the germs, our aim should be to maintain the nutrition of every part of the body at its highest point.   To do this two things are necessary:

1. A supply of nutritive material sufficient to replace what is consumed in developing the energies of the body and to provide a surplus for increase or growth of the body.

2. The proper use or exercise of the body.

We speak now only of the second, and especially in its relation to the proper use of the lungs.

When a muscle contracts it squeezes the blood out of its veins laden with waste products, which are to be removed ultimately from the body, and a flood of fresh arterial blood carrying nutritive material is poured into the muscular tissue.   The circulation of the organ is improved, effete matters gotten rid of, and the nutrition and vitality rise.   The lung tissue itself is not muscular, and depends for its proper aeration upon the action of the respiratory muscles.   The aeration of the lungs improves the circulation in them in a manner analogous to that of the muscle.   With improved circulation comes improved nutrition and increased resistance to injurious influences. A collapsed and atrophied lung that receives but little of the life-giving blood constantly invites disease. The functions of the lungs and heart are the fundamental functions of the body. Upon them the welfare of all the other functions depends. It should be the aim of educational gymnastics to develop these fundamental functions; and any system which neglects this is imperfect and injurious.

Breathing is carried on without conscious effort on our part; it is automatic. Waking or sleeping, the muscles which expand the chest alternately and rhythmically contract and relax, and it is impossible for us to cease to breathe by mere exercise of will, except for a very short time. If the modern man lived in a physiologically correct environment the automatism of the respiratory function would do its work thoroughly and perfectly. But civilized life involves so many departures from an ideal hygienic condition that it has become necessary to teach the modern man even how to breathe. Occupation, clothes, dwellings, and numerous other conditions incident to life among crowds combine to bring about this effect.

At each inspiration every part of the lungs should receive a fresh supply of air. To do this necessitates a full, though not a forcible, expansion of the chest; therefore anything that restricts the free play of the chest should be discarded, and any position that brings pressure upon the chest or abdomen avoided. The cavity of the chest containing the lungs is enlarged in all its diameters by the lifting of the ribs and the descent of the muscular partition, the diaphragm, which shuts it off from the abdominal cavity. The mere elevation of the ribs is enabled to enlarge the chest in both its antero-posterior and transverse diameters by virtue of their peculiar curves, and the angle at which they articulate with the vertebral column. The diaphragm is a muscular wall forming the floor of the chest cavity; it is dome-shaped, with its convexity upward. In *in*spiration it contracts, the dome descends and flattens, thus enlarging the chest cavity in its perpendicular diameter. Much nonsense has been written about the action of the diaphragm, and astonishing ignorance displayed by writers of pretentious works on elocution and physical culture. I have repeatedly seen it stated in such books that the diaphragm is a muscle of *ex*piration. This is not true. The diaphragm is solely a muscle of *in*spiration; it is perfectly passive in *ex*piration. At the end of inspiration the muscles relax, the

ribs fall, the diaphragm ascends, the chest cavity is lessened, the air is expelled from the
lungs. All this occurs without muscular effort,
and by the recoil of the lungs alone. The lungs
are elastic, they are continually on the stretch,
and when the expanding chest-wall ceases to
pull upon them they contract, drawing with
them the chest-wall and diaphragm. It is only
in forced breathing that muscular action has
any part in expiration.

By training we can impress upon the respiratory apparatus deranged by injurious influences a habit of correct action. The study of
elocution involves this training and the conse-
quent development, and in this lies its chief
value; for refinement and culture are ever the
possession of the few, but physical (also moral)
superiority benefits the race and state as a
whole. Exercises that tend to the development
of the respiratory apparatus are given in the
body of this book.

Where disease has already obtained a foothold
certain modifications of method are necessary
to be followed in training before the average
health is re-established. These modifications
form a branch by themselves, called Medical
Gymnastics, which can only be treated of in a
work upon Therapy.

HYGIENE OF SCHOOL LIFE.

From the first glimmer of reason the child is constantly receiving impressions through every sense. The accumulated impressions make the moral and mental character. Training, therefore, should begin in the cradle.

The time at which it is proper to send a child to school should not be judged by the age, by the intellectual development, or by the eagerness to learn. No one factor should determine such an important step, but the whole being should be looked at and primary importance given to the physical development. The child has its whole life to study and learn, but it has only the first ten years or so to lay the foundation of a long life of health and happiness. I must strongly protest against the pernicious custom of sending children from the cradle to the school-room, which often results in producing those melancholy examples of the blindness of parental pride, infant prodigies, but more frequently in stunted mind and body in place of intellectual and physical strength.

In the first decade of life let them vegetate. If possible, turn them into the woods and fields, to rub up against Nature and learn to love her; have sight, hearing, touch, every sense sharpened and trained as no other teacher can train them. The kindergarten system in a manner obviates this necessity of keeping children so long from school, for in it the tasks are light, of a pleasant nature, and liberally interlarded with exercise and play. Too much cannot be said in praise of this method when intelligently carried out.

The selection of a school should be made with care and forethought. What studied attention, or even worry, will a mother give to the woollen clothes of her child, weighing the effect on complexion, figure, etc.; but how often does chance or convenience dictate the choice of the weavers of that child's mental trappings, or mind garments, which are but seldom or never renewed. As I am speaking to Catholics it is not necessary to plead the cause of the soul in education (the mind is looked after by all who give education any thought); it is my part to call attention to the claims of the body. "With stupidity and sound digestion man may front much." I do not wish to disparage mental brilliancy, but to accentuate the relationship between health and material happiness. See therefore that the school to which the boy or girl is sent is one wherein the body as well as the mind is trained. Make it your business to inquire concerning the sanitary condition of the

buildings, the arrangements for drainage, heat-
ing, and, above all, for light and air. The relations of air to life are constantly ignored in our
schools and churches. The architect strives
for effect, the builder for cheapness, and the
end and object of the structure seems too frequently lost sight of.

The school is made by the student, it exists
only for the student, and in every detail the
student should first be considered. Whether
ignorance or parsimony be the cause, it is certain that when parents and guardians insist
upon these conditions they will be fulfilled.

I will briefly consider the hygiene of school
life under four heads, not to lay down rules, but
merely to indicate the lines along which this
study is to be pursued.

Food.—Foods are divided into three great
classes: carbohydrates, proteids, and fats. Bread,
vegetables, fruits, etc., are equivalent to carbohydrates; flesh of animals, milk, eggs, are equivalent to proteids; butter, lard, etc., to fats. The
diet should contain enough of these three kinds
of food to replace the waste of the tissues and to
supply material for growth. The proportion of
nitrogenous (proteid) to non-nitrogenous (carbohydrates and fats) should be about 1:3.
These are best obtained by mixed feeding.

Vegetarianism is a delusion. The human alimentary canal is not adapted for the digestion of the large masses of food necessarily ingested when vegetables alone are used. There is no particular class of food which is peculiarly adapted to the student's needs; the brain-building properties of certain foods (e.g., fish) are imaginary. In health and where adequate exercise is taken, the ordinary mixed diet fulfils all indications. Where sufficient exercise is not taken, with almost any diet digestive disorders (the skirmish line of disease) are apt to appear, and they are invited and fostered by the bakery, where the student, both male and female, delights to feast upon pies, cakes, cream puffs, and other dietetic horrors. Going from the table back immediately to the desk is the source of many differences between the mind and the stomach. Insufficient supply of water is also one of the most common mistakes, especially among girls. The function of water in the body is a most important one, and a well-defined group of disorders owe their origin in great part to a lack of this fluid. About three pints a day is the proper quantity, and it is best taken pure. Without going into detail in the matter, it may be said that any one doing active work requires more nitrogenous (proteid) matter than one at rest, and that children and women require less than men. But it should be noted that a healthy growing boy may consume and require more than an adult man. Variety of diet is essential to the proper maintenance of nutrition; even milk, which is an ideal food, containing everything necessary to supply waste, if fed upon exclusively for too long a time, will produce emaciation and loss of strength. The amount and character of food required at different periods of life have been mathematically calculated, but such tables have a very limited application. Every one is a law unto himself, and the body makes known its wants, which the intelligent can perceive. For the boy or girl at school, then, a plain mixed diet, avoiding pastry and confectionery, prohibiting tea and coffee and highly-seasoned foods until fourteen, and for liquid milk and a liberal quantity of water. It would be wrong to close a paragraph on alimentation without mentioning the importance of regularity in the excretory functions.

Air.—The relations of air to life and health are most intimate. Oxygen, its life-giving constituent, enters into the minute blood corpuscles in the lung, and is distributed by the circulating blood to every cell in the body. To deprive a person of a sufficient quantity of oxygen deranges not only the lungs and circulatory organs, but every part of the body; every cell and fibre, from the delicate brain cell, with its marvellous properties, to the solid bone that supports him, feels that loss. When air is breathed by a person he not only takes oxygen from it, but he adds to it carbonic acid and certain organic matters which he exhales from the lungs; the skin also gives to the surrounding air a part of its excreta. This air, which has been once respired, is not only useless for human beings, but it is positively poisonous. Its most harmful properties are not due to the carbonic acid, but to the organic matters thrown off from the lungs. There is a curious indifference to impure air; very dainty people, who could not touch a plate of soup in which they had seen the waiter's thumb immersed, do not object to taking into their lungs the foul, poisonous air which has been in and out of numerous other people, perhaps dirty, perhaps diseased.

There should be provided for every occupant of a room about 3000 cubic feet of fresh air every hour. In addition to this, every ordinary gas burner consuming three feet of gas per hour necessitates a supply of 5400 cubic feet of fresh air.

In a small room with numerous occupants this requires so frequent a renewal of the air

that it is difficult or even impossible to secure
that change without draughts. Good ventilation
does not mean draughts, generally speaking. If
the cubic space per head is increased, the fre-
quency of the change of air may be reduced. A
space of 750 to 1000 cubic feet per head should
be provided for in an apartment, and then a
change of air three or four times an hour can be
effected without draughts. In private dwellings
efficient ventilation is not a difficult problem;
the porosity of the walls, minute crevices, open
fires etc., are generally capable of maintaining
a fairly pure atmosphere. In schools with
crowded classrooms, stupidly arranged, it is difficult. Every school should have a system of artificial ventilation, of which there are several
quite successful. Where this is lacking, and in
old buildings, the attention of those in charge
should be constantly directed to the atmosphere
of the classrooms. By opening small spaces of
a number of windows instead of one window
widely, or, better, by inserting a piece of plank
three or four inches wide beneath the lower
sash, which allows of the entrance of air through
the space between the two sashes, where it is directed upward and a draught avoided, some
ventilation can be obtained. Never ventilate
rooms from the hall, but always the hall from

the rooms. The recesses or changes of class
should be arranged so that the classrooms are
emptied and an opportunity given to flood them
with fresh air several times a day. The teacher
who gives a little attention to these things will
soon note the improvement if she has before
marked the drooping heads, the drowsy eyes, the
growing listlessness of the pupils as the day
lengthens, the result, not of mental labor, but of
the carbonized atmosphere. In the sleeping-
rooms the same care should be taken to secure
a constant supply of fresh air, and the popular
fear of the night air should be put aside; after
the sun goes down there is no air but night air.
During sleep the whole body is recruited, and
oxygen is a prime factor in this rehabilitation of
the tissues and storing up of energy. Children
should be induced to give their lungs a chance;
air is about the only thing that is free, and
though draughts and exposure are sometimes
pernicious, the coddling plan is infinitely more
so. The dangers of a dust-laden atmosphere
were hinted at when speaking of tuberculosis.

Exercise and Play.—The folly of developing
but one side of the body would be apparent; that
of developing but one side of the being is as sense-
less. The body must be cultivated if we would
raise up men and women whose life is not a bur-

den and who are worthy and capable of perpetu-
ating the nation.

Physical exercise may be divided into that
which is taken within doors, in gymnasia or
classrooms, and that which is taken in the
field or on the water. The latter is by far the
more preferable. The element of enjoyment is
greater, and the subtle forces of nature seem to
infuse themselves into the being and expand it
with life. For a large number the indoor exercises only are practicable. There are many systems of gymnastics, simple and elaborate. All
contain something good, but the Swedish system
of Ling is probably the best. It is arranged to
meet an essential and general educational purpose, and is adaptable to existing educational
institutions. It does not try to develop physical
specialists, but only to train the different organs
of the body in a manner that they may serve the
great double purpose of promoting the efficiency
of the circulatory and respiratory functions and
of increasing the volitional control of the whole
body. To perceive the benefit to be derived from
gymnastics one need only state a few familiar
facts. Whether necessary or not, the pupils
have been doing their work in a sitting posture,
the chest more or less contracted, the upper part
of the body leaning forward against the desk,

the thorax bent forward and downward, pressing downward upon the abdominal organs, and somewhat checking the venous circulation of these organs. This state of injurious muscular repose has continued for hours. As a consequence we have these results: A more or less temporary passive congestion, or tendency to congestion of the brain and abdominal organs; restricted action of the chest, decreased respiration, the general tone of the muscles lowered, and the mind tired from prolonged concentration. The first object of the exercises must be to counteract these evils, to relieve the brain and the oppressed organs, to reinstate a healthy respiration and circulation, to tone up the body generally, at the same time giving attention to the educational purpose of the exercises. The power of mental concentration agrees with a curve that rises steadily for one hour and then gradually falls. After one hour, with the average pupil, it is spurring a jaded steed; therefore, at the end of every hour there should be some interruption of class work, a change of class, recess, or exercise. At least in these formative years play should alternate with work, and that play which involves physical exercise is the most desirable. Hence the value of athletic sports, which no amount of gymnasium work can replace. The tendency to overdo these should be restrained by proper authority, and all exercise, in and out of doors, should, where possible, be under the supervision of a medical director, who would ascertain the needs of each student and prescribe for him the kind and amount of exercise fitted to his case. Where means are limited, a few simple movements can be studied and taught by any teacher, and without any apparatus the condition and working power of a class can be wonderfully improved.

Study.—The greater part of the pupil's time is, unfortunately, spent in the study of books. Study should be pursued according to the dictates of hygienic law. We should strive to get the maximum amount of profit with the minimum expenditure of vital energy. A great many spend more time learning how to study than they do in acquiring a knowledge of their subjects. But that is the teacher's affair. The proper duration of continued study must be determined for each individual by observation. It varies greatly. In no case should study be continued to the point of mental exhaustion. At all times harmful, this is especially injurious when the study is done at night, for the over-tired brain refuses to rest, and insomnia results. The period of the day most favorable to study also varies with the individual. The usual advice is to get up early and study in the morning. To those who study best at that time it is good advice, to others it is nonsense.

The curve of mental power is found to reach its highest point in the middle of the afternoon. So on physiological grounds alone the morning is not the best time for study.

The care of the eyes is one of the most important and one of the most neglected branches of the hygiene of school life. Reading should never be allowed where there is not a good light, which should fall upon the page and not upon the eyes. It is frightful to think of the frequent mischief to eyesight that has been caused by the neglect at schools of the most elementary requisites to protect it from unnecessary strain, such as an abundance of light coming from a proper direction, and desks so shaped that the book or paper is supported squarely before the reader.

The stupid want of care in providing these essentials to eye-comfort has gone far towards converting the educated classes into short-sighted classes.

The position of the body during the hours at the desk should receive attention. Cramped, sidelong, or lolling positions interfere with respiration and circulation, and in young bodies tend to produce deformities. Girls when they slide sideways into benches often allow their skirts to be heaped up under one hip, tilting the pelvis, and producing a compensating curve of the spine which may be made permanent. A seat that will discourage lolling, etc., does not mean an uncomfortable seat. If any educator thinks he is stimulating cerebral activity by placing the pupil upon a hard, comfortless bench with a back most aggressively knobby he is grievously mistaken.

Next to abuse of the eyes "cramming" for examinations is productive of most ill. In young girls it is especially pernicious, and often results in shattering their nervous systems for life. If I were ignorant of the school calendar I could tell when examinations were at hand by the number of cases of chorea (St. Vitus' dance) which come to my clinic at that time. There is no defence for "cramming," for knowledge gained in that manner is never retained but for a short time.

At present examinations seem to be a necessary evil, but the science and art of pedagogy is advancing rapidly, and soon I hope we will look back upon examinations as we now look upon torture.

PRINTED BY BENZIGER BROTHERS, NEW YORK.

STANDARD CATHOLIC BOOKS

PUBLISHED BY

BENZIGER BROTHERS,

CINCINNATI:	NEW YORK:	CHICAGO:
343 MAIN ST.	36 & 38 BARCLAY ST.	211-213 MADISON ST.

DOCTRINE, INSTRUCTION, DEVOTION.

ABANDONMENT; or, Absolute Surrender of Self to Divine Providence. Rev. J. P. Caussade, S.J. _net_, 0 40

ADORATION OF THE BLESSED SACRAMENT. Tesnière. Cloth, _net_, 1 25

ALPHONSUS LIGUORI, ST. Complete Ascetic Works. 22 vols., each, _net_, 1 25

ANALYSIS OF THE GOSPELS. Rev. L. A. Lambert, LL.D. _net_, 1 25

APOSTLES' CREED, THE. Rev. Müller, C.SS.R. _net_, 1 10

ART OF PROFITING BY OUR FAULTS. Rev. J. Tissot. _net_, 0 40

BIBLE, THE HOLY. 0 80

BIRTHDAY SOUVENIR. Mrs. A. E. Buchanan. 0 50

BLESSED VIRGIN, THE. Rev. Dr. Keller. 0 75

BLOSSOMS OF THE CROSS. Emily Giehrl. 1 25

BOOK OF THE PROFESSED.
Vol. I. _net_, 0 75
Vol. II. _net_, 0 60
Vol. III. _net_, 0 60

BOYS' AND GIRLS' MISSION BOOK. By the Redemptorist Fathers.
0 35
Per 100, 17 50

CATECHISM EXPLAINED, THE. Spirago-Clarke. _net_, 2 50

CATHOLIC BELIEF. Faa di Bruno.
Paper, *0.25; 100 copies, 15 00
Cloth, *0.50; 25 copies, 7 50

CATHOLIC CEREMONIES and Explanation of the Ecclesiastical Year. Abbé Durand.
Paper, *0.30; 25 copies, 4 50
Cloth, *0.60; 25 copies. 9 00

CATHOLIC PRACTICE AT CHURCH AND AT HOME. Rev. Alex. L. A. Klauder.
Paper, *0.30; 25 copies, 4 50
Cloth, *0.60; 25 copies, 9 00

CATHOLIC TEACHING FOR CHILDREN. Winifride Wray.   0 40

CATHOLIC WORSHIP. Rev. R. Brennan, LL.D.
    Paper, *0.15; 100 copies,   10 00
    Cloth, *0.25; 100 copies,   17 00

CHARACTERISTICS OF TRUE DEVOTION. Rev. N. Grou, S.J.
             net, 0 75

CHARITY THE ORIGIN OF EVERY BLESSING.   0 60

CHILD OF MARY. Prayer-Book.   0 60

CHILD'S PRAYER-BOOK OF THE SACRED HEART.   0 20

CHRISTIAN FATHER. Right Rev. W. Cramer.   •
    Paper, *0.25; 25 copies,   3 75
    Cloth, *0.40; 25 copies,   6 00

CHRISTIAN MOTHER. Right Rev. W. Cramer.
    Paper, *0.25; 25 copies,   3 75
    Cloth, *0.40; 25 copies,   6 00

CHURCH AND HER ENEMIES. Rev. M. Müller, C.SS.R. net, 1 10

COMEDY OF ENGLISH PROTESTANTISM. A. F. Marshall. net, 0 75

COMPLETE OFFICE OF HOLY WEEK.   0 50
    100 copies,   25 00

COMMUNION. ⎫   ⎧ Per 100, net, 3 50
CONFESSION. ⎬ Edited by   ⎨ Per 100, net, 3 50
CONFIRMATION. ⎭ Rev. John J. Nash, D.D. ⎩ Per 100, net, 3 50

DEVOTION OF THE HOLY ROSARY and the Five Scapulars. net, 0 75

DEVOTIONS AND PRAYERS FOR THE SICK-ROOM. Krebs, C.SS.R.
    Cloth,   net, 1 00

DEVOTIONS AND PRAYERS OF ST. ALPHONSUS. A Complete Prayer-
    book.   1 00

DEVOTIONS TO THE SACRED HEART for the First Friday of Every
    Month. By Père Huguet.   0 40

DEVOUT INSTRUCTIONS, GOFFINE'S. 1.00; 25 copies,   17 50

DIGNITY AND DUTY OF THE PRIEST; or, Selva, a Collection of
    Material for Ecclesiastical Retreats. By St. Alphonsus de
    Liguori.   net, 1 25

DIGNITY, AUTHORITY, DUTIES OF PARENTS, ECCLESIASTICAL AND
    CIVIL POWERS. By Rev. M. Müller, C.SS.R.   net, 1 40

DIVINE OFFICE: Explanations of the Psalms and Canticles. By
    St. Alphonsus de Liguori.   net, 1 25

EPISTLES AND GOSPELS. 0.25; 100 copies,   19 00

EUCHARIST AND PENANCE. Rev. M. Müller, C.SS.R.   net, 1 10

EUCHARISTIC CHRIST, Reflections and Considerations on the
    Blessed Sacrament. Rev. A. Tesnière.   net, 1 00

EUCHARISTIC GEMS. A Thought About the Most Blessed Sac-
    rament for Every Day in the Year. By Rev. L. C. Coel-
    enbier.   0 75

EXPLANATION OF COMMANDMENTS, ILLUSTRATED.   1 00

EXPLANATION OF THE APOSTLES' CREED, ILLUSTRATED.   1 00

EXPLANATION OF THE BALTIMORE CATECHISM OF CHRISTIAN DOC-
    TRINE. Rev. Th. L. Kinkead.   net, 1 00

EXPLANATION OF THE COMMANDMENTS, Precepts of the Church.
    Rev. M. Müller, C.SS.R.   • net, 1 10

EXPLANATION OF THE GOSPELS and of Catholic Worship. Rev. L.
A. Lambert.
   Paper, *0.30; 25 copies,   4 50
   Cloth, *0.60; 25 copies,   9 00
EXPLANATION OF THE HOLY SACRAMENTS, ILLUSTRATED.   1 00
EXPLANATION OF THE HOLY SACRIFICE OF THE MASS. Rev. M.
v. Cochem.   1 25
EXPLANATION OF THE OUR FATHER AND THE HAIL MARY. Rev.
R. Brennan, LL.D.   0 75
EXPLANATION OF THE PRAYERS AND CEREMONIES OF THE MASS,
ILLUSTRATED. Rev. D. I. Lanslots, O.S.B.   1 25
EXPLANATION OF THE SALVE REGINA. Liguori.   0 75
EXTREME UNCTION.   0 10
   100 copies,   6 00
FAMILIAR EXPLANATION OF CATHOLIC DOCTRINE. Rev. M.
Müller, C.SS.R.   1 00
FIRST AND GREATEST COMMANDMENT. By Rev. M. Müller, C.SS.R.
                                 net, 1 40
FIRST COMMUNICANT'S MANUAL.   .   0 50
   100 copies,   25 00
FLOWERS OF THE PASSION. Thoughts of St. Paul of the Cross.
By Rev. Louis Th. de Jésus-Agonisant. 0.50; per 100
copies,   30 00
FOLLOWING OF CHRIST. Thomas à Kempis.
   With Reflections, 0.50; 100 copies,   25 00
   Without Reflections, 0.45; 100 copies,   22 50
   Edition de luxe,   1 50
FOUR LAST THINGS, THE: Death, Judgment, Heaven, Hell. Med-
itations. Father M. v. Cochem. Cloth,   0 75
GARLAND OF PRAYER. With Nuptial Mass. Leather,   0 90
GENERAL CONFESSION MADE EASY. Rev. A. Konings, C.SS.R.
   Flexible. 0.15; 100 copies,   10 00
GENERAL PRINCIPLES OF THE RELIGIOUS LIFE. Verheyen, O.S.B.
                                  net, 0 30
GLORIES OF DIVINE GRACE. Dr. M. J. Scheeben.   *net*, 1 50
GLORIES OF MARY. St. Alphonsus de Ligouri. 2 vols., *net*, 2 50
GOFFINE'S DEVOUT INSTRUCTIONS. 140 Illustrations. Cloth, 1 00
   25 copies,   17 50
GOLDEN SANDS. Little Counsels for the Sanctification and Hap-
piness of Daily Life.
   Third Series,   0 50
   Fourth Series,   0 50
   Fifth Series,   0 50
GRACE AND THE SACRAMENTS. By Rev. M. Müller, C.SS.R.
                                 net, 1 25
GREAT MEANS OF SALVATION AND OF PERFECTION. St. Alphonsus
de Liguori.   *net*, 1 25
GREAT SUPPER OF GOD, THE. A Treatise on Weekly Communion.
By Rev. S. Coubé, S.J. Edited by Rev. F. X. Brady, S.J.
Cloth,   *net*, 1 00
GREETINGS TO THE CHRIST-CHILD, a Collection of Poems for the
Young. Illustrated.   0 60

LABORS OF THE APOSTLES, Their Teaching of the Nations. By Right Rev. L. de Goesbriand, D.D., Bishop of Burlington.
net, 1 00

LETTERS OF ST. ALPHONSUS DE LIGUORI. 4 vols., each vol.,
net, 1 25

LETTERS OF ST. ALPHONSUS LIGUORI and General Alphabetical Index to St. Alphonsus' Works. *net*, 1 25

LITTLE BOOK OF SUPERIORS. *net*, 0 60

LITTLE CHILD OF MARY. A Small Prayer-book. 0.35; 100 copies,
21 00

LITTLE MANUAL OF ST. ANTHONY. Illustrated. 0.60; 100 copies,
36 00

LITTLE MONTH OF MAY. By Ella McMahon. Flexible, 0 25
100 copies, 19 00

LITTLE MONTH OF THE SOULS IN PURGATORY. 0.25; 100 copies,
19 00

LITTLE OFFICE OF THE IMMACULATE CONCEPTION. 0.05; per 100,
2 50

LITTLE PRAYER-BOOK OF THE SACRED HEART. By Blessed Margaret Mary Alacoque. 0 40

MANIFESTATION OF CONSCIENCE. Langogne, O.M.Cap. *net*, 0 50

MANUAL OF THE BLESSED VIRGIN. Complete Manual of Devotion of the Mother of God. 0 60

MANUAL OF THE HOLY EUCHARIST. Conferences on the Blessed Sacrament and Eucharistic Devotions. By Rev. F. X. Lasance. 0 75

MANUAL OF THE HOLY FAMILY. 0 60

MARIAE COROLLA. Poems by Father Edmund of the Heart of Mary, C.P. Cloth, 1 25

MASS DEVOTIONS AND READINGS ON THE MASS. By Rev. F. X. Lasance. Cloth, 0 75

MAXIMS AND COUNSELS OF ST. FRANCIS DE SALES. *net*, 0 35

MAY DEVOTIONS, NEW. Rev. Augustine Wirth, O.S.B. *net*, 1 00

MEANS OF GRACE. By Rev. Richard Brennan, LL.D. 2 50

MEDITATIONS FOR ALL THE DAYS OF THE YEAR. By Rev. M. Hamon, S.S. 5 vols., *net*, 5 00

MEDITATIONS FOR EVERY DAY IN THE YEAR. Baxter. *net*, 1 25

MEDITATIONS FOR EVERY DAY IN THE YEAR. Rev. B. Vercruysse. S.J. 2 vols., *net*, 2 75

MEDITATIONS FOR RETREATS. St. Francis de Sales. Cloth, net, 0 75

MEDITATIONS ON THE FOUR LAST THINGS. Father M. v. Cochem.
0 75

MEDITATIONS ON THE LAST WORDS FROM THE CROSS. Father Charles Perraud. *net*, 0 50

MEDITATIONS ON THE LIFE, THE TEACHINGS, AND THE PASSION OF JESUS CHRIST. Ilg-Clarke. 2 vols., *net*, 3 50

MEDITATIONS ON THE MONTH OF OUR LADY. 0 75
MEDITATIONS ON THE PASSION OF OUR LORD. 0.40; 100 copies,
24 00

MISCELLANY. Historical sketch of the Congregation of the Most Holy Redeemer. Rules and Constitutions of the Congregation of the Most Holy Redeemer. Instructions on the Religious State. By St. Alphonsus de Liguori. *net,* 1 25

MISSION BOOK FOR THE MARRIED. Very Rev. F. Girardey, C.SS.R. 0.50; 100 copies, 25 00

MISSION BOOK FOR THE SINGLE. Very Rev. F. Girardey, C.SS.R. 0.50; 100 copies, 25 00

MISSION BOOK OF THE REDEMPTORIST FATHERS. A Manual of Instructions and Prayers to Preserve the Fruits of the Mission. Drawn chiefly from the works of St. Alphonsus Liguori. 0.50; 100 copies, 25 00

MISTRESS OF NOVICES, THE, Instructed in Her Duties. Leguay. *net,* 0 75

MOMENTS BEFORE THE TABERNACLE. Rev. Matthew Russell, S.J. *net,* 0 40

MONTH, NEW, OF ST. JOSEPH. St. Francis de Sales. 0 25

MONTH, NEW, OF THE HOLY ANGELS. St. Francis de Sales. 0 25
100 copies, 19 00

MONTH, NEW, OF THE SACRED HEART. St. Francis de Sales. 0 25

MONTH OF MAY; a Series of Meditations on the Mysteries of the Life of the Blessed Virgin. B. F. Debussi, S.J. 0 50

MONTH OF THE DEAD; or, Prompt and Easy Deliverance of the Souls in Purgatory. By Abbé Cloquet. 0 50

MOST HOLY ROSARY. Thirty-one Meditations. Right Rev. W. Cramer, D.D. 0 50

MOST HOLY SACRAMENT. Rev. Dr. Jos. Keller. 0 75

MY FIRST COMMUNION: The Happiest Day of My Life. Brennan. 0 75

NEW RULE OF THE THIRD ORDER. 0.05; per 100, 3 00

NEW TESTAMENT, Cheap Edition.
32mo, flexible cloth, *net,* 0 15
32mo, lambskin, limp, round corners, gilt edges, *net,* 0 75

NEW TESTAMENT. Illustrated Edition.
24mo, garnet cloth, with 100 full-page illustrations, *net,* 0 60
24mo, Rutland Roan, limp, round corners, red or gold edges, *net,* 1 25

NEW TESTAMENT. India Paper Edition.
3003 Lambskin, limp, round corners, gilt edges, *net,* 1 00
4011 Persian Calf, limp, round corners, gilt edges, *net,* 1 25
4017 Morocco, limp, round corners, gilt edges, gold roll inside, *net,* 1 50

NEW TESTAMENT. Large Print Edition.
12mo, cloth, round corners, red edges, *net,* 0 75
12mo, American seal, limp, round corners, red or gold edges, *net,* 1 50

NEW TESTAMENT STUDIES. By Right Rev. Mgr. Thomas J. Conaty, D.D. 12mo, 0 60

OFFICE, COMPLETE, OF HOLY WEEK. 0.50; 100 copies, 25 00

ON THE ROAD TO ROME. By W. Richards. *net,* 0 50

OUR BIRTHDAY BOUQUET. E. C. Donnelly. 1 00

OUR LADY OF GOOD COUNSEL IN GENAZZANO. Mgr. Geo. F. Dillon, D.D. o 75

OUR FAVORITE DEVOTIONS. By Very Rev. Dean A. A. Lings. o 60

OUR FAVORITE NOVENAS. Very Rev. Dean A. A. Lings. o 60

OUR MONTHLY DEVOTIONS. By Very Rev. Dean A. A. Lings. 1 25

OUR OWN WILL AND HOW TO DETECT IT IN OUR ACTIONS. Rev. John Allen, D.D. *net*, o 75

PARACLETE, THE. Devotions to the Holy Ghost. o 60

PARADISE ON EARTH OPEN TO ALL; A Religious Vocation the Surest Way in Life. By Rev. Antonio Natale, S.J. *net*, o 40

PASSION AND DEATH OF JESUS CHRIST. By St. Alphonsus de Liguori. *net*, 1 25

PASSION FLOWERS. Poems by Father Edmund, of the Heart of Mary, C.P. 1 25

PEARLS FROM THE CASKET OF THE SACRED HEART. Eleanor C. Donnelly. o 50

PEOPLE'S MISSION BOOK, THE. Paper, 0.10; per 100, 6 00

PERFECT RELIGIOUS, THE. De la Motte. Cloth, *net*, 1 00

PICTORIAL LIVES OF THE SAINTS. New, very cheap edition, with Reflections for Every Day in the Year. 1.00; 25 copies, 17 50

PIOUS PREPARATION FOR FIRST HOLY COMMUNION. Rev. F. X. Lasance. Cloth, o 75

POPULAR INSTRUCTIONS ON MARRIAGE. Very Rev. F. Girardey, C.SS.R. Paper, 0.25; 25 copies, 3 75
Cloth, 0.40; 25 copies, 6 00

POPULAR INSTRUCTIONS ON PRAYER. By Very Rev. Ferreol Girardey, C.SS.R. Paper, 0.25; 25 copies, 3 75
Cloth, 0.40; 25 copies, 6 00

POPULAR INSTRUCTIONS TO PARENTS on the Bringing Up of Children. By Very Rev. F. Girardey, C.SS.R. Paper, 0.25;
25 copies, 3 75
Cloth, 0.40; 25 copies, 6 00

PRAYER-BOOK FOR LENT. Gethsemani, Jerusalem, and Golgotha. Rev. A. Geyer. o 50

PRAYER. The Great Means of Obtaining Salvation. By St. Alphonsus de Liguori. o 50

PREACHING. Vol. XV. St. Alphonsus de Liguori. The Exercises of the Missions. Various Counsels. Instructions on the Commandments and Sacraments. *net*, 1 25

PREPARATION FOR DEATH. St. Alphonsus de Liguori. Considerations on the Eternal Truths. Maxims of Eternity. Rule of Life. *net*, 1 25

PRODIGAL SON; or, The Sinner's Return to God. *net*, 1 00

REASONABLENESS OF CATHOLIC CEREMONIES AND PRACTICES. Rev. J. J. Burke. o 35

RELIGIOUS STATE, THE. With a Treatise on the Vocation to the Priesthood. By St. Alphonsus de Liguori. o 50

REVELATIONS OF THE SACRED HEART to Blessed Margaret Mary. Bougaud. Cloth, *net*, 1 50

7

SACRAMENTALS OF THE HOLY CATHOLIC CHURCH. Rev. A. A. Lambing, D.D. Paper, 0.30; 25 copies, 4 50
    Cloth, 0 60; 25 copies, 9 00
SACRAMENTALS—Prayer, etc. Rev. M. Müller, C.SS.R. *net*, 1 00
SACRED HEART, THE. Rev. Dr. Joseph Keller. 0 75
SACRED HEART, THE. Studies in the Sacred Scriptures. Rev. H. Saintrain, C.SS.R. *net*, 2 00
SACRIFICE OF THE MASS WORTHILY CELEBRATED, THE. Rev. Father Chaignon, S.J. *net*, 1 50
SECRET OF SANCTITY. St. Francis de Sales. *net*, 1 00
SERAPHIC GUIDE, THE. A Manual for the Members of the Third Order of St. Francis. By a Franciscan Father. 0 60
SHORT CONFERENCES ON THE LITTLE OFFICE OF THE IMMACULATE CONCEPTION. Very Rev. J. Rainer. 0 50
SHORT STORIES ON CHRISTIAN DOCTRINE. From the French by Mary McMahon. *net*, 0 75
SPIRITUAL CRUMBS FOR HUNGRY LITTLE SOULS. Mary E. Richardson. 0 50
SPIRITUAL DIRECTION. *net*, 0 60
SPIRITUAL EXERCISES FOR A TEN DAYS' RETREAT. Very Rev. v. Smetana, C.SS.R. *net*, 1 00
SODALISTS' VADE MECUM. 0 50
SONGS AND SONNETS. Maurice Francis Egan. 1 00
SOUVENIR OF THE NOVITIATE. Rev. Edward I. Taylor. *net*, 0 60
ST. ANTHONY. Rev. Dr. Jos. Keller. 0 75
ST. JOSEPH, OUR ADVOCATE. Father Huguet. 0 90
STATIONS OF THE CROSS. Illustrated. 0 50
STORIES FOR FIRST COMMUNICANTS. Rev. J. A. Keller, D.D. 0 50
STRIVING AFTER PERFECTION. Rev. Joseph Bayma, S.J. *net*, 1 00
SURE WAY TO A HAPPY MARRIAGE. Rev. Edward I. Taylor. Paper, 0.25; 25 copies, 3 75
    Cloth, 0.40; 25 copies, 6 00
THOUGHT FROM BENEDICTINE SAINTS. *net*, 0 35
THOUGHT FROM ST. ALPHONSUS. *net*, 0 35
THOUGHT FROM ST. FRANCIS OF ASSISI and His Saints. *net*, 0 35
THOUGHT FROM ST. IGNATIUS. *net*, 0 35
THOUGHTS FROM ST. TERESA. *net*, 0 35
THOUGHT FROM ST. VINCENT DE PAUL. *net*, 0 35
THOUGHTS AND COUNSELS for the Consideration of Catholic Young Men. Rev. P. A. Döss, S. J. *net*, 1 25
TRUE POLITENESS. Abbé Francis Demore. *net*, 0 60
TRUE SPOUSE OF JESUS CHRIST. St. Alphonsus de Liguori. 2 vols., Centenary Edition, *net*, 2 50
    The same in 1 volume, *net*, 1 00
TWO SPIRITUAL RETREATS FOR SISTERS. Rev. E. Zollner. *net*, 1 00
VENERATION OF THE BLESSED VIRGIN. Her Feasts, Prayers, Religious Orders, and Sodalities. Rev. B. Rohner, O.S.B. 1 25

VICTORIES OF THE MARTYRS; or, The Lives of the Most Celebrated Martyrs of the Church. Vol. IX. Alphonsus de Liguori.
net, 1 25

VISITS TO JESUS IN THE TABERNACLE. Hours and Half-Hours of Adoration before the Blessed Sacrament. With a Novena to the Holy Ghost and Devotions for Mass, Holy Communion, etc. Rev. F. X. Lasance. Cloth,
1 25

VISITS TO THE MOST HOLY SACRAMENT and to the Blessed Virgin Mary. St. Alphonsus de Liguori. '
0 50

VOCATIONS EXPLAINED: Matrimony, Virginity, The Religious State, and the Priesthood. By a Vincentian Father.
0 10
100 copies,
6 00

WAY OF INTERIOR PEACE. Rev. Father De Lehen, S.J. *net*, 1 25

WAY OF SALVATION AND PERFECTION. Meditations, Pious Reflections, Spiritual Treatises. St. Alphonsus de Liguori. *net*, 1 25

WAY OF THE CROSS. Paper, 0.05; 100 'copies,
2 50

WORDS OF WISDOM. A Concordance to the Sapiential Books. Edited by Rev. John J. Bell.
net, 1 25

YEAR OF THE SACRED HEART. A Thought for Every Day of the Year. Anna T. Sadlier.
0 50

YOUNG GIRLS' BOOK OF PIETY, AT SCHOOL AND AT HOME. A Prayer-book for Girls in Convent Schools and Academies. Golden Sands.
1 00

JUVENILES.

ADVENTURES OF A CASKET.	0 45
ADVENTURES OF A FRENCH CAPTAIN.	0 45
AN ADVENTURE WITH THE APACHES. Gabriel Ferry.	0 40
ANTHONY. A Tale of the Time of Charles II. of England.	0 45
ARMORER OF SOLINGEN. William Herchenbach.	0 40
BERTHA; or, Consequences of a Fault.	0 45
BETTER PART.	0 45
BISTOURI. A. Melandri.	0 40
BLACK LADY, AND ROBIN RED BREAST. Canon Schmid.	0 25
BLANCHE DE MARSILLY.	0 45
BLISSYLVANIA POST-OFFICE. Marion Ames Taggart.	0 40
BOYS IN THE BLOCK. Maurice F. Egan.	0 25
BRIC-A-BRAC DEALER.	0 45
BUZZER'S CHRISTMAS. Mary T. Waggaman.	0 25
BY BRANSCOME RIVER. Marion Ames Taggart.	0 40
CAKE AND THE EASTER EGGS. Canon Schmid.	0 25
CANARY BIRD. Canon Schmid.	0 40
CAPTAIN ROUGEMONT.	0 45
CASSILDA; or, The Moorish Princess.	0 45
CAVE BY THE BEECH FORK, THE. Rev. H. S. Spalding, S.J. Cloth,	0 85
COLLEGE BOY, A. Anthony Yorke. Cloth,	0 85
CONVERSATIONS ON HOME EDUCATION.	0 45

OVERSEER OF MAHLBOURG. Canon Schmid. 0 25
PANCHO AND PANCHITA. Mary E. Mannix. 0 40
PAULINE ARCHER. Anna T. Sadlier. 0 40
PICKLE AND PEPPER. Ella Loraine Dorsey. 0 85
PRIEST OF AUVRIGNY. 0 45
QUEEN'S PAGE. Katharine Tynan Hinkson. 0 40
RICHARD; or, Devotion to the Stuarts. 0 45
ROSE BUSH. Canon Schmid. 0 25
SEA-GULL'S ROCK. J. Sandeau. 0 40
SUMMER AT WOODVILLE. Anna T. Sadlier. 0 40
TALES AND LEGENDS OF THE MIDDLE AGES. F. De Capella. 0 75
TAMING OF POLLY. Ella Loraine Dorsey. 0 85
THREE GIRLS AND ESPECIALLY ONE. Marion A. Taggart. 0 40
THREE LITTLE KINGS. Emmy Giehrl. 0 25
TOM PLAYFAIR; or, Making a Start. Father Finn. 0 85
TOM'S LUCKPOT. Mary T. Waggaman. 0 40
TREASURE OF NUGGET MOUNTAIN. M. A. Taggart. 0 85
VILLAGE STEEPLE, THE. 0 45
WINNETOU, THE APACHE KNIGHT. Marion Ames Taggart. 0 85
WRONGFULLY ACCUSED. William Herchenbach. 0 40

NOVELS AND STORIES.

ASER. THE SHEPHERD. A Christmas Story. Marion Ames Taggart. *net*, 0 35
BEZALEEL. A Christmas Story. Marion Ames Taggart. *net*, 0 35
CIRCUS RIDER'S DAUGHTER, THE. A Novel. F. v. Brackel. 1 25
CONNOR D'ARCY'S STRUGGLES. A Novel. Mrs. W. M. Bertholds. 1 25
DION AND THE SIBYLS. A Classic Novel. Miles Keon. Cloth, 1 25
FABIOLA; or, The Church of the Catacombs. By Cardinal Wiseman. Popular Illustrated Edition, 0.90; Edition de luxe, 5 00
FABIOLA'S SISTERS. A Companion Volume to Cardinal Wiseman's "Fabiola." A. C. Clarke. 1 25
HEIRESS OF CRONENSTEIN, THE. Countess Hahn-Hahn. 1 25
IDOLS; or, The Secrets of the Rue Chaussée d'Antin. De Navery. 1 25
LET NO MAN PUT ASUNDER. A Novel. Josephine Marié 1 00
LINKED LIVES. A Novel. Lady Gertrude Douglas. 1 50
MARCELLA GRACE. A Novel. Rosa Mulholland. Illustrated Edition. 1 25
MISS ERIN. A Novel. M. E. Francis. 1 25
MONK'S PARDON, THE. A Historical Novel of the Time of Philip IV. of Spain. Raoul de Navery. 1 25
MR. BILLY BUTTONS. A Novel. Walter Lecky. 1 25
OUTLAW OF CAMARGUE, THE. A Novel. A. de Lamothe. 1 25

PASSING SHADOWS. A Novel. Anthony Yorke. 1 25

PERE MONNIER'S WARD. A Novel. Walter Lecky. 1 25

PETRONILLA. E. C. Donnelly. 1 00

PRODIGAL'S DAUGHTER, THE. Lelia Hardin Bugg. 1 00

ROMANCE OF A PLAYWRIGHT. Vte. Henri de Bornier. 1 00

ROUND TABLE OF THE REPRESENTATIVE AMERICAN CATHOLIC NOVELISTS. Complete Stories, with Biographies, Portraits, etc. Cloth, 1 50 .

ROUND TABLE OF THE REPRESENTATIVE FRENCH CATHOLIC NOVELISTS. Complete Stories, with Biographies, Portraits, etc. Cloth, 1 50

ROUND TABLE OF THE REPRESENTATIVE IRISH AND ENGLISH CATHOLIC NOVELISTS. Complete Stories, Biographies, Portraits, etc. Cloth, 1 50

TRUE STORY OF MASTER GERARD, THE. By Anna T. Sadlier. 1 25

VOCATION OF EDWARD CONWAY. A Novel. Maurice F. Egan. 1 25

WOMAN OF FORTUNE, A. Christian Reid. 1 25

WORLD WELL LOST. Esther Robertson. 0 75

LIVES AND HISTORIES.

AUTOBIOGRAPHY OF ST. IGNATIUS LOYOLA. Edited by Rev. J. F. X. O'Conor. Cloth, *net,*. 1 25 .

BLESSED ONES OF 1888, THE. Bl. Clement Maria Hofbauer, C.SS.R.; Bl. Louis Marie Grignon de Montfort; Bl. Brother Aegidius Mary of St. Joseph; Bl. Josephine Mary of St. Agnes. From the original by Eliza A. Donnelly. With Illustrations, 0 50

HISTORIOGRAPHIA ECCLESIASTICA quam Historiae seriam Solidamque Operam Navantibus, Accommodavit Guil. Stang, D.D. *net,* 1 00

HISTORY OF THE CATHOLIC CHURCH. Brueck. 2 vols. *net,* 3 00

HISTORY OF THE CATHOLIC CHURCH. John Gilmary Shea, LL.D. 1 50

HISTORY OF THE PROTESTANT REFORMATION IN ENGLAND AND IRELAND. Wm. Cobbett. Cloth, *net,* 0.50; paper, *net,* 0 25

LETTERS OF ST. ALPHONSUS LIGUORI. Rev. Eugene Grimm, C.SS.R. Centenary Edition. 5 vols., each, *net,* 1 25

LIFE OF BLESSED MARGARET MARY. Mgr. Bougaud, Bishop of Laval. *net,* 1 50

LIFE OF CHRIST. Illustrated. Father M. v. Cochem. 1 25

LIFE OF FATHER CHARLES SIRE, of the Society of Jesus. Rev. Vital Sire. *net,* 1 00

LIFE OF FATHER JOGUES. Missionary Priest of the Society of Jesus. Father F. Martin, S.J. *net,* 0 75

LIFE OF FR. FRANCIS POILVACHE, C.SS.R. Paper, *net,* 0 20

LIFE OF MOTHER FONTBONNE, Foundress of the Sisters of St. Joseph of Lyons. Abbé Rivaux. Cloth, *net,* 1 25

LIFE OF SISTER ANNE KATHERINE EMMERICH, of the Order of St. Augustine. Rev. Thomas Wegener, O.S.A. *net,* 1 50

LIFE OF ST. ALOYSIUS GONZAGA, of the Society of Jesus.
Rev. J. F. X. O'Conor, S.J. *net*, 0 75
LIFE OF ST. CATHARINE OF SIENA. Edward L. Aymé, M.D. 1 00.
1 00
LIFE OF ST. CLARE OF MONTEFALCO. Locke, O.S.A. *net*, 0 75
LIFE OF THE BLESSED VIRGIN. Illustrated. Rev. B. Rohner,
O.S.B. 1 25
LIFE OF THE VEN. MARY CRESCENTIA HOESS. Rev. C. Dey-
mann, O.S.F. *net*, 1 25
LITTLE LIVES OF SAINTS FOR CHILDREN. Berthold. Ill. Cloth,
0 75
LOURDES: Its Inhabitants, Its Pilgrims, Its Miracles. Rev.
R. F. Clarke, S.J. 0 75
NAMES THAT LIVE IN CATHOLIC HEARTS. Anna T. Sadlier. 1 00
OUR BIRTHDAY BOUQUET. Eleanor C. Donnelly. 1 00
OUR LADY OF GOOD COUNSEL IN GENAZZANO. A History of that
Ancient Sanctuary. Anne R. Bennett-Gladstone. 0 75
OUTLINES OF JEWISH HISTORY, from Abraham to Our Lord.
Rev. F. E. Gigot, S.S. *net*, 1 50
OUTLINES OF NEW TESTAMENT HISTORY. Rev. F. E. Gigot,
S.S. Cloth, *net*, 1 50
PICTORIAL LIVES OF THE SAINTS. Cloth, 1.00; 25 copies, 17 50
REMINISCENCES OF RT. REV. EDGAR P. WADHAMS, D.D., First
Bishop of Ogdensburg. Rev. C. A. Walworth. *net*, 1 00
ST. ANTHONY, THE SAINT OF THE WHOLE WORLD. Rev. Thomas
F. Ward. Cloth, 0 75
STORY OF THE DIVINE CHILD. Very Rev. Dean A. A. Lings. 0 75
VICTORIES OF THE MARTYRS. St. Alphonsus de Liguori. *net*, 1 25
VISIT TO EUROPE AND THE HOLY LAND. Rev. H. Fairbanks. 1 50
WIDOWS AND CHARITY. Work of the Women of Calvary and Its
Foundress. Abbé Chaffanjon. Paper, *net*, 0 50
WOMEN OF CATHOLICITY. Anna T. Sadlier. 1 00

THEOLOGY, LITURGY, SERMONS, SCIENCE, AND PHILOSOPHY.

ABRIDGED SERMONS, for All Sundays of the Year. St. Al-
phonsus de Liguori. Centenary Edition. Grimm, C.SS.R.
net, 1 25
BAD CHRISTIAN, THE. Rev. F. Hunolt, S.J. Translated by
Rev. J. Allen, D.D. 2 vols., *net*, 5 00
BLESSED SACRAMENT, SERMONS ON THE. Especially for the Forty
Hours' Adoration. Rev. J. B. Scheurer, D.D. Edited
by Rev. F. X. Lasance. *net*, 1 50
BREVE COMPENDIUM THEOLOGIAE DOGMATICAE ET MORALIS una
cum, aliquibus Notionibus Theologiae Canonicae Liturgiae,
Pastoralis et Mysticae, ac Philosophiae Christianae. Berthier,
M.S. *net*, 2 50
BUSINESS GUIDE FOR PRIESTS. Stang, D.D. *net*, 0 85
CANONICAL PROCEDURE IN DISCIPLINARY AND CRIMINAL CASES
OF CLERICS. Rev. F. Dröste. *net*, 1 50
CHILDREN OF MARY, SERMONS FOR THE. From the Italian of
Rev. F. Callerio. Edited by Rev. R. F. Clarke, S.J. *net*, 1 50
CHRISTIAN ANTHROPOLOGY. Sermons. Rev. John Thein. net, 2 50
CHRISTIAN PHILOSOPHY. A Treatise on the Human Soul.
Rev. J. T. Driscoll, S.T.L. *net*, 1 25

CHRISTIAN'S LAST END, THE. Sermons. Rev. F. Hunolt, S.J. Translated by Rev. J. Allen, D.D. 2 vols., *net,* 5 00
CHRISTIAN'S MODEL, THE. Sermons. Rev. F. Hunolt, S.J. Translated by Rev. J. Allen, D.D. 2 vols., *net,* 5 00
CHRISTIAN STATE OF LIFE, THE. Sermons. Rev. F. Hunolt, S.J. Translated by Rev. J. Allen, D.D. *net,* 5 00
CHRIST IN TYPE AND PROPHECY. Rev. A. J. Maas, S.J., Professor of Oriental Languages in Woodstock College. 2 vols., *net,* 4 00
CHURCH ANNOUNCEMENT BOOK. *net,* 0 25
CHURCH TREASURER'S PEW. Collection and Receipt Book. *net,* 1 00
COMMENTARIUM IN FACULTATES APOSTOLICAS EPISCOPIS necnon Vicariis et Praefectis Apostolicis per Modum Formularum concedi solitas ad usum Venerabilis Cleri, imprimis Americani concinnatum ab Antonio Konings, C.SS.R. Edito quarto, recognita in pluribus emendata et aucta, curante Joseph Putzer, C.SS.R. *net,* 2 25
COMPENDIUM JURIS CANONICI, ad usum Cleri et Seminariorum hujus Regionis accommodatum. *net,* 2 00
COMPENDIUM SACRAE LITURGIAE JUXTA RITUM ROMANUM una cum Appendice de Jure Ecclesiastico Particulari in America Foederata Sept. vigente scripsit P. Innocentius Wapelhorst, O.S.F. Editio quinta emendatior. *net,* 2 50
CONFESSIONAL, THE. Right Rev. A. Roeggl, D.D. *net,* 1 00
DATA OF MODERN ETHICS EXAMINED. Ming, S.J. *net,* 2 00
DE PHILOSOPHIA MORALI PRAELECTIONES quas in Collegio Georgiopolitano Soc. Jesu, Anno 1889-90 Habuit P. Nicolaus Russo. Editio altera. *net,* 2 00
ECCLESIASTICAL DICTIONARY. Rev. John Thein. *net,* 5 00
ELEMENTS OF ECCLESIASTICAL LAW. Rev. S. B. Smith, D.D.
  ECCLESIASTICAL PERSONS. *net,* 2 50
  ECCLESIASTICAL PUNISHMENTS. *net,* 2 50
  ECCLESIASTICAL TRIALS. *net,* 2 50
FUNERAL SERMONS. Rev. Aug. Wirth, O.S.B. 2 vols., *net,* 2 00
GENERAL INTRODUCTION TO THE STUDY OF HOLY SCRIPTURES. Rev. Francis E. Gigot, S.S. Cloth, *net,* 2 00
GOD KNOWABLE AND KNOWN. Rev. Maurice Ronayne, S.J. *net,* 1 25
GOOD CHRISTIAN, THE. Rev. J. Allen, D.D. 2 vols., *net,* 5 00
HISTORY OF THE MASS AND ITS CEREMONIES IN THE EASTERN AND WESTERN CHURCH. Rev. John O'Brien. *net,* 1 25
LAST THINGS, SERMONS ON THE FOUR. Hunolt. Translated by Rev. John Allen, D.D. 2 vols., *net,* 5 00
LENTEN SERMONS. Edited by Rev. Augustine Wirth, O.S.B. *net,* 2 00
LIBER STATUS ANIMARUM; or, Parish Census Book. *Pocket Edition, net,* 0.25; half leather, *net,* 2 00
LITERARY, SCIENTIFIC, AND POLITICAL VIEWS OF ORESTES A. BROWNSON. H. F. Brownson. *net,* 1 25
MARRIAGE PROCESS IN THE UNITED STATES. Smith. *net,* 2 50
MORAL PRINCIPLES AND MEDICAL PRACTICE, THE BASIS OF MEDICAL JURISPRUDENCE. Rev. Charles Coppens, S.J., Professor of Medical Jurisprudence in the John A. Creighton Medical College, Omaha, Neb.; Author of Text-books in Metaphysics, Ethics, etc. *net,* 1 50
NATURAL LAW AND LEGAL PRACTICE. Holaind, S.J. *net,* 1 75

14

NATURAL THEOLOGY. Rev. B. Boedder, S.J. *net*, 1 50

NEW AND OLD SERMONS. A Repertory of Catholic Pulpit Eloquence. Edited by Rev. Augustine Wirth, O.S.B. 8 vols., *net*, 16 00

OFFICE OF TENEBRAE, THE. Transposed from the Gregorian Chant into Modern Notation. Rev. J. A. McCallen, S.S. *net*, 0 50

OUR LORD, THE BLESSED VIRGIN, AND THE SAINTS. SERMONS ON. Rev. Francis Hunolt, S.J. Translated by Rev. John Allen, D.D. 2 vols., *net*, 5 00

OUTLINES OF DOGMATIC THEOLOGY. Rev. Sylvester Jos. Hunter, S.J. 3 vols., *net*, 4 50

OUTLINES OF NEW TESTAMENT HISTORY. Gigot. Cloth, *net*, 1 50

PASTORAL THEOLOGY. Rev. Wm. Stang, D.D. *net*, 1 50

PENANCE, SERMONS ON. Rev. Francis Hunolt, S.J. Translated by Rev. John Allen. 2 vols., *net*, 5 00

PENITENT CHRISTIAN, THE. Sermons. Rev. F. Hunolt. Translated by Rev. John Allen, D.D. 2 vols., *net*, 5 00

PEW-RENT RECEIPT BOOK. *net*, 1 00

PRAXIS SYNODALIS. Manuale Synodi Diocesanae ac Provincialis Celebrandae. *net*, 0 60

PRIEST IN THE PULPIT, THE. A Manual of Homiletics and Catechetics. Rev. B. Luebbermann. *net*, 1 50

REGISTRUM BAPTISMORUM. *net*, 3 50

REGISTRUM MATRIMONIORUM. *net*, 3 50

RITUALE COMPENDIOSUM seu Ordo Administrandi quaedam Sacramenta et alia Officia Ecclesiastica Rite l'eragendi ex Rituali Romano, novissime edito desumptas. *net*, 0 75

ROSARY, SERMONS ON THE MOST HOLY. Frings. *net*, 1 00

SACRED HEART, SIX SERMONS ON DEVOTION TO THE. Rev. Dr. E. Bierbaum. *net*, 0 60

SANCTUARY BOYS' ILLUSTRATED MANUAL. Embracing the Ceremonies of the Inferior Ministers at Low Mass, High Mass, Solemn High Mass, Vespers, Asperges, Benediction of the Blessed Sacrament, and Absolution for the Dead. Rev. J. A. McCallen, S.S. *net*, 0 50

SERMON MANUSCRIPT BOOK. *net*, 2 00

SERMONS FOR THE SUNDAYS AND CHIEF FESTIVALS OF THE ECCLESIASTICAL YEAR. With Two Courses of Lenten Sermons and a Triduum for the Forty Hours. Rev. J. Pottgeisser, S.J. 2 vols., *net*, 2 50

SERMONS ON THE CHRISTIAN VIRTUES. Rev. F. Hunolt, S.J. Translated by Rev. John Allen. 2 vols., *net*, 5 00

SERMONS ON THE DIFFERENT STATES OF LIFE. Rev. F. Hunolt, S.J. Translated by Rev. John Allen. 2 vols., *net*, 5 00

SERMONS ON THE SEVEN DEADLY SINS. Rev. F. Hunolt, S.J. 2 vols. Translated by Rev. John Allen, D.D. *net*, 5 00

SHORT SERMONS. Rev. F. Hunolt, S.J. 5 vols., 10 00

SHORT SERMONS FOR LOW MASSES. Schouppe, S.J. *net*, 1 25

SYNOPSIS THEOLOGIAE DOGMATICAE AD MENTEM S. THOMAE AQUINATIS, hodiernis moribus accommodata, auctore Ad. Tanquerey, S.S.:

1. THEOLOGIA FUNDAMENTALIS. Half morocco, *net*, 1 50
2. THEOLOGIA DOGMATICA SPECIALIS. 2 vols., half morocco, *net*, 3 00

15

THEOLOGIA MORALIS NOVISSIMI ECCLESIAE DOCTORIS ALPHONSI. In Compendium Redacta, et Usui Venerabilis Cleri Americani accommodata. Auctore Rev. A. Konings, C.SS.R. Editio septima, auctior et novis curis expolitior curante Henrico Kuper, C.SS.R. 2 vols., *net*, 4 00

TWO-EDGED SWORD. Rev. Augustine Wirth, O.S.B. Paper, *net*, 0 25

VADE MECUM SACERDOTUM, continens Preces ante et post Missam, modum providendi infirmos, necnon multas Benedictionum Formulas. Cloth, *net*, 0 25; Morocco flexible, *net*, 0 50

WHAT CATHOLICS HAVE DONE FOR SCIENCE. With sketches of the Great Catholic Scientists. Rev. Martin S. Brennan. 1 00

MISCELLANEOUS.

A GENTLEMAN. M. F. Egan, LL.D. 0 75

A LADY. Manners and Social Usages. Lelia Hardin Bugg. 0 75

AIDS TO CORRECT AND EFFECTIVE ELOCUTION. With Selected Readings. Eleanor O'Grady. 1 25

BONE RULES; or, Skeleton of English Grammar. Rev. J. B. Tabb, A.M. 0 50

CANTATA CATHOLICA. B. H. F. Hellebusch. *net*, 2 00

CATECHISM OF FAMILIAR THINGS. Their History, and the Events which Led to Their Discovery. With a Short Explanation of Some of the Principal Natural Phenomena. 1 00

CATHOLIC HOME ANNUAL. Stories by Best Writers. 0 25

CORRECT THING FOR CATHOLICS, THE. Lelia Hardin Bugg. 0 75

ELOCUTION CLASS. A Simplification of the Laws and Principles of Expression. Eleanor O'Grady. *net*, 0 50

EVE OF THE REFORMATION, THE. An Historical Essay on the Religious, Literary, and Social Condition of Christendom, with Special Reference to Germany and England, from the Beginning of the Latter Half of the Fifteenth Century to the Outbreak of the Religious Revolt. Rev. Wm. Stang. Paper, *net*, 0 25

GAMES OF CATHOLIC AMERICAN AUTHORS:

PICTORIAL GAME OF CATHOLIC AMERICAN AUTHORS.
Series A, *net*, 0 15
Series B, *net*, 0 15

GAMES OF QUOTATIONS FROM CATHOLIC AMERICAN AUTHORS.
Series I., *net*, 0 15
Series II., *net*, 0 15
Series III., *net*, 0 15

GUIDE FOR SACRISTANS and Others Having Charge of the Altar and Sanctuary. By a Member of an Altar Society. *net*, 0 75

HOW TO GET ON. Rev. Bernard Feeney. 1 00

LITTLE FOLKS' ANNUAL. 0.05; per 100, 3 00

ON CHRISTIAN ART. Edith Healy. 0 50

READINGS AND RECITATIONS FOR JUNIORS. O'Grady. *net*, 0 50

SELECT RECITATIONS FOR CATHOLIC SCHOOLS AND ACADEMIES. Eleanor O'Grady. 1 00